CONTENTS

Published by Runpast Publishing, Cheltenham 1996

Printed by The Amadeus Press Ltd., Huddersfield.
Typesetting and reproduction by Viners Wood Associates, Painswick, Glos.

ISBN 1 870754 41 7

No.3031 *Achilles* at Didcot. Built in 1894 it was the first of this class of express passenger locomotive.

CHAPTER ONE

Introduction to Didcot

As I sat in a compartment of the 8.55am ex Worcester on 11 October 1939, being whisked across the Cotswolds by a 'Castle' class loco, there was ample time to reflect and to absorb the scenery speeding by and to imagine what was happening on the footplate of the loco, which, for the past four years, I had polished with care and pride.

I had plenty of time to muse over the new life which was before me. My thoughts were constantly focused on one particular aspect, and one question remained in my mind. What will Didcot be like? This query had pervaded ever since my chargeman cleaner gave me orders to report to Didcot for promotion as fireman. Dick, the chargeman, was apologetic for giving me the orders to go away on my own. Three of my cleaning colleagues were all reporting to Banbury together. Dick thought that seemed unfair; so did I but, in retrospect, it was I who was the lucky one.

'Where's Didcot?' I asked him.

'I'm not sure where it is, somewhere up by London I think.'

After muttering something in his nasal tones he said:

'Let's go down to the office and find out.'

Fortunately, a driver who worked to London came along to explain; it was then that I remembered changing trains there on my way back home after a medical exam, over four years previously. Try as I may, I was quite unable to recall anything of what I might have seen, almost as if Didcot had been banished from my mind.

Having changed at Oxford into a slow train and stopping at small wayside stations I had the impression of going deeper into the country and away from home at Worcester, with its old Victorian station, the brick buildings inlaid with glazed tiles, ornate canopies over the platforms and unusually large disc signals suspended from the canopy girders giving it a singular appearance.

Worcester loco shed was odd in the extreme, in fact there were two sheds, one for passenger engines, the other for goods with a shunting yard in between. The sheds were dirty and very sooty, dark and dingy, lit by gas lamps which failed to light the sheds with the yellow light they gave. The sheds were crowded in on two sides by very high embankments, elsewhere all around were wagons, filling the sidings. Factory buildings belonging to the railway were scattered about and the tall goods shed stood in the middle of it all. Then there was the office of the divisional

superintendent loftily built in a position from which the whole scene could be surveyed.

Nothing moved very fast at Worcester by nature of the track with its various speed restrictions – there was an atmosphere almost of lethargy, things happening at their own pace, but for the urgency of the London bound trains.

My first impressions upon arrival at Didcot, by comparison, were of an open station, fairly new and tidy, standing higher than the road on one side and being surrounded on three sides by open country. I liked this, my old home was on the edge of the city, only a few houses separating us from the country.

From the station platform I could see across to the loco shed, it was almost new and stood out clean and free from soot beyond the rows of passenger train sidings. Nothing was moving, it was eleven o'clock, the morning shift had completed its task for the time being. The whole place seemed serene.

As I stood on the platform wondering how I should get on to the shed, an express train hurried through on the main line at great speed towards London, my first sight of a fast train at close quarters. Then my train moved away towards Reading, leaving me feeling quite alone. A porter directed me to the shed via the subway and across the footboards, from there I made my way along the ash pit where the engine fires were dropped, past the coaling stage and on to the office.

The station had, in the past, seen various alterations both to its superstructure and track layout, the most recent being carried out between 1930-33, but generally regarded as 1932 when the major work was completed, hence the new appearance.

In the aftermath of the First World War the country had witnessed the worst depression for many years; the railways went into a steep decline. In the past the railways had been instrumental in the development of communities throughout the country.

Didcot was somewhat different, it had neither industry nor population to stimulate its growth, in fact little was known of its existence outside the parameters of the Church of England, the Oxford colleges and the local landowners, who between them, had previously owned all the land in and around Didcot.

The depression culminated in the bitter General Strike

Didcot station c1910 as seen from the West End signal box looking east. The departing train is leaving the down Oxford platform towards Swindon. The two up lines are on the left.

Oxford County Libraries (Didcot)

6

of 1926, which forced the government to take action to create employment for the many who were now out of work. To this end the railways were offered a deal in the way of tax concessions, on condition that they spent money improving stations, trains and facilities in general.

The work was authorised under the Developments (Loans, Guarantees and Grants) Act 1929. Major G.R.S. Wilson and Col A.H.L. Mount were appointed and ordered to inspect the completed work at Didcot on 25 July 1933.

A sum of money in excess of £8,000,000 was allocated to the GWR to cover various projects throughout the whole system, from marshalling yards, goods depots, doubling of lines, carriage shops and engine sheds with extension of the automatic train control system and also improvements to several stations.

Didcot was not particularly run down. So why was it chosen for refurbishment? With so little advantageous local income during this period, the answer can only lie in its importance as a major junction. From the outset, when Brunel built the station, it had been blessed with four roads, these had been retained through various minor alterations. The down main line ran through the station on its southern side. To make the junction to the north a crossover was laid at the east end to allow trains to cross over to the adjoining line with the platform on the right hand side. From here trains could leave directly for the north. In effect this arrangement put two down lines side by side. The up main line ran on the other side of the centre platform, crossing the northern junction at the west end. The up Oxford line came into the station next to the up main – two up lines together.

As traffic grew this layout proved to be self defeating, delays occurred as a consequence of the crossing movements at each end of the station and also prevented through running on the up main line. The only real benefit of this arrangement was that passengers alighting on the centre platform were able to cross the platform to connect with other trains.

The quadrupling of the line from London to Didcot was commenced in 1892 the first section being completed from Didcot as far as the new station at Cholsey and Moulsford in April 1892, first opened for goods trains 27 December the same year. On 30 July 1893 the last section from Reading to Pangbourne was opened, completing the four roads from Westbourne Park through to Didcot. The down and up main lines were now positioned on the southern side with the relief lines on the northern side, except at Didcot, where the two down lines were left as they were, on the southern side.

The decision to continue the up and down main lines together through the station as far as Foxhall junction, with the new relief lines alongside was the reason for the major alterations which took place. The work undertaken during these alterations did little to alter the appearance of the station, except for the Oxford line platform which was extended eastwards and an additional line laid on its northern side to serve stopping trains both to Oxford and Reading.

The three junctions at East End, West End and Foxhall were all relaid, each of which had a new signal box built to cope with the extra levers required.

The Traffic Committee meeting of 30 April 1931 authorised 'the provision of three new signal boxes to be erected by Hinkins & Frewin Ltd with an additional payment of £212.5.0.' The boxes were of a new design first used in 1923 which led to the type nine design of which very few were built between 1927/33, with a steel frame and concrete blocks to fill in, some of which were rendered. The three erected at Didcot were not finished in this way. The estimated cost of the type nine box was £650 against £870 for the conventional brick built type.

Although the three boxes were of a standard design they were each of a different length, according to the frame size in use: Foxhall had 76 levers, West End 88, and East junction 150. They each had seven or eight spare levers.

A new crossover was laid from down main to down relief and from there the junction was taken to the avoiding line to North junction, with equivalent up lines. The Oxford line junction from the new down relief stayed in much the same position, and with the connection to Oxford removed from the original down Oxford (now the new up main) the main line platform was extended towards Foxhall. The junction there was completely changed as it now became the end of the relief line, as well as the junction to the north.

These new junctions required re-signalling and several gantries were used to simplify the operations.

The final report by the Board of Trade (BOT) inspectors commenced with the reasons for the alterations:

The facilities in question have been provided to improve operation over this heavily trafficked section of the Company's main line, including the quadrupling of the main lines through the station and a new locomotive depot; quadrupling between Wantage Road and Challow making four track stations; also at Shrivenham.

The report continued in a detailed manner on every aspect of the work, stating:

The layout has been entirely remodelled, and the existing locomotive depot has been transferred to a site further to the north-west with a new depot of standard type, with a turntable and elevated coal road.

Of the platforms it states:

The down main is extended by 167ft, the island platform by 230ft and the faces of the platforms are straight. The relief lines are curved to a radius of 74¼ chains. The new island platform 810ft long with the Oxford side curve to a radius of 49½ chains.

The original subway has been widened to 14ft except where the original width of 8ft is retained (beyond stairways). New stairways to both island platforms are provided; no alteration to the down main. (This suggests that the down main line stairway is original.) Lifts have been provided to all platforms with a capacity of 1½ tons.

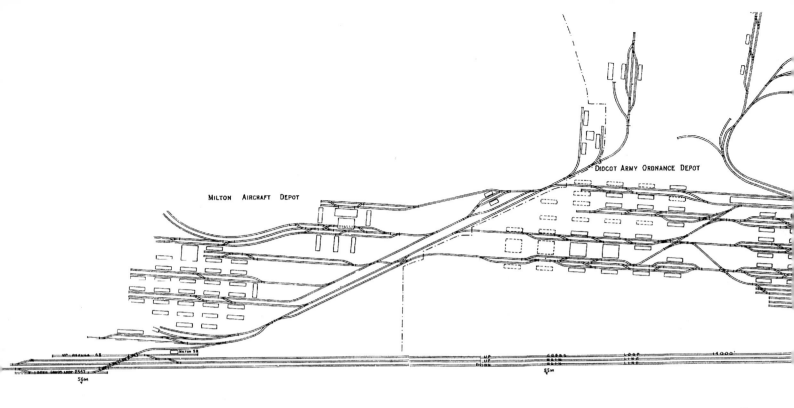

Overall plan of Didcot together with the Army and RAF depots c1920. The crossovers and leads into the RAF at Milton are still in place at this time.
GWR publication

Didcot yard full with wagons is typical of the busy period of the 1920s. The provender stores stands high alongside the railway to the west of the station with the hay barn to the rear.
Oxford County Libraries (Didcot)

Facing page: A 1920s view of the station looking west. The train on the left is standing on the down Oxford line with a shunter attending the rear. The train across the platform is on the up main line with the up Oxford line on its right. Sidings and the loco shed can be seen to the right.
Author's collection

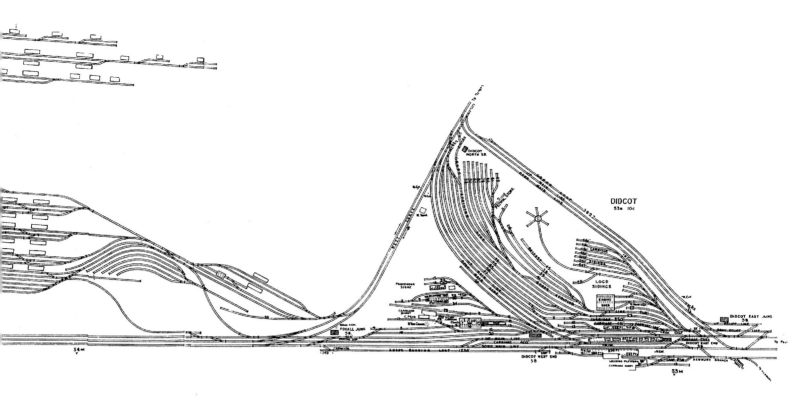

G.W.R. Junction, Didcot, Berks.

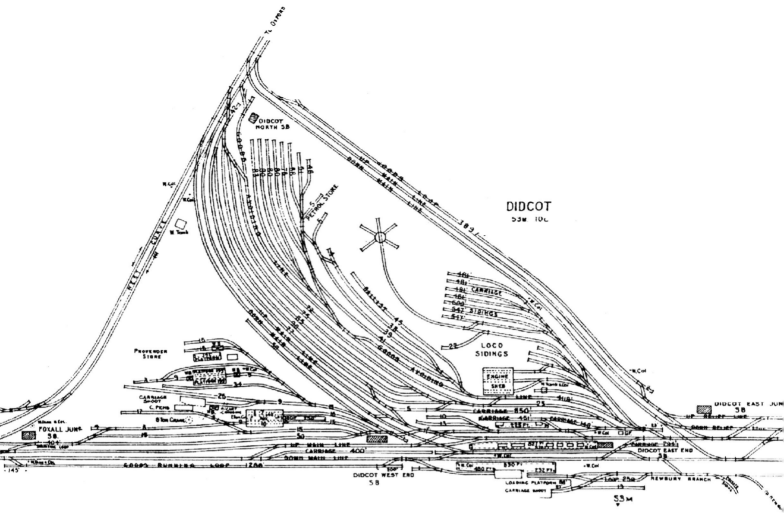

Enlarged detail of Didcot station area.

No.3528, previously No.3211, waits in the carriage sidings. Rebuilt from an 0-4-4T in June 1900, the loco was withdrawn in July 1927.
Real Photographs Co. Ltd.

GWR Steam Rail Motor No.85 with trailer working between Didcot and Reading. It was withdrawn in the late 1920s.

Brian Davis collection

The main improvement to the track was the laying of junctions at East junction with a speed of 40mph – the highest crossover speed allowed at this time – the remainder of the crossovers were restricted to 15 or 20mph. Track circuits were also installed to improve working safety.

The old carriage shed was demolished to make way for the new loco shed with its modern facilities and lifting shop.

Spacious sidings were laid to accommodate the passenger stock, and at the same time the centre goods yards were not overlooked, they were greatly increased in capacity, and the operating staff had much improved accommodation.

Although the BOT inspectors were detailed to carry out their inspection on 25 July 1933 it was not until 24/25 February 1935 that they actually visited Didcot. This is quite surprising when one considers the reason for inspection is to ensure that all work carried out regarding track and signalling has been completed to a satisfactory safety standard. During this delay of almost two years the new works were being used without official authority.

The business at the station had seen fluctuating fortunes as the records over the period from 1903 will show:

	Staff (all grades)	Pay bills	Total passenger receipts
1903	120	£8,332	£18,152
1926	143	£23,552	£92,835
1930	143	£25,767	£86,549
1933	139	£23,568	£84,235
1938	153	£27,961	£168,730

During the same period, goods traffic receipts were 1903 – £7,196 1926 – £59,901 1930 – £49,967 1933 – £47,523 1938 – £109,072.

The figures show that from the years of depression all receipts fell on the goods side until the dramatic increase in 1938; passenger receipts remained somewhat constant. The rebuilding had no bearing upon this, only that the new layout would have made it easier to handle.

It was to this somewhat prosperous situation that I arrived to take up my position as a fireman in 1939. The number of locomen at that time was forty-five sets to cover the working of twenty locos.

On my arrival I reported to the time office and was then asked to wait in the stores for a call-boy to take me out to find lodgings. While waiting in the stores a diminutive man wearing a suit came by, and stopping for a few moments, asked:

'Have you just arrived here?'

To which I simply replied 'Yes.'

He then said:

'So have I, ain't it a bloody hole.'

After enquiring from where I had come, he left me. The store keeper, standing by and having heard the encounter asked:

'Did you know who that man was? He's the new shed master, Mr Young.'

Although we both had arrived on the same day there was a vast difference in our status, Mr Young was the most senior man at the shed while I was at the opposite end of the scale, the most junior.

I was given my turn of duty for the next day, an afternoon turn they told me, to give me chance to settle in.

I booked on duty next day and wondered who the driver would be. A well built man in his early forties came along and said 'I believe you are along with me – wait here, I'll be back in a minute.' Bert East was his name, we got along very well together, in fact, I have always believed that it was his friendship and influence which settled me into my new life. We joined up with two other sets of men and walked for what seemed ages before arriving at the ordnance depot to relieve one of the pilot engines shunting the depot.

The following week it was an early turn on the yard pilot. Here was a difference, there was activity all around. Where we shunted up and down at the rear of the station, with the passenger sidings and the loco shed on the other side of us, I was able to take in all that moved.

The station was constantly busy, at all times someone was moving about. Trains came in from all directions, passengers boarding and alighting, going down to the subway to change trains at another platform. The activity was at times bewildering, I was unable to sort out in my mind just what was happening. I asked Bert so many questions I think he got a bit fed up, saying:

'Don't worry, I'll tell you all about it in good time.'

It wasn't only where the trains came from and went to but what all the signals were for, I had not been used to seeing so many.

Most of the day the station was exceptionally busy, trains called from all directions, north, south, east and west, including South Wales. Most of the main line trains were met by trains from the Oxford line to make connections, often an up and a down train arriving together, their passengers scurrying down the subway in a heaving mass of humanity, pushing and shoving for fear of missing their connections.

This was normally quite unnecessary as most trains in those times were booked as much as ten minutes at a junction station such as Didcot. The express services usually had a guard's van at each end of the train which pressed the porters hard to complete their work, without causing delay, at times this was difficult to avoid, the heavy four-wheeled station barrows had to be trundled along the platform to the lifts and back up again to another platform; Didcot didn't have crossing boards at the ends of the platforms as did most stations. In addition to passengers' luggage and parcels there was always a large consignment of Royal Mail to be handled.

Trains arriving from the West Country invariably carried loaded milk churns. These were normally tilted on one side by the porter and rolled at an angle on to a waiting barrow, providing one was readily available. If not, the churn was eased down to the platform where it landed with a thud onto its protective ring round the base. Each churn which landed a bit too hard in this way, cut an arc shaped scar in the platform coping stone. After many years of this it was quite easy to see where the guards vans had continuously stopped, the area was well scarred.

There were some twenty to twenty-five porters on duty during the daytime, even then they were hard pushed to cope with several trains at a time. The porters varied in age, most of them I recall were rather elderly, some still sporting heavy moustaches, reminiscent of the Victorian era. The younger men were of military age, many of whom were called up for service to be replaced by female staff.

These men worked in such close proximity to us but in general there was no contact between them and the locomen, never any real reason to do so; almost as if we worked for a different company.

A long time elapsed before I was made aware of who the station master was. He was a very quiet unassuming man, short and stocky. He wore a hat and dark pin-striped suit when he eventually ventured out of his office to come up to the platform; he seemed quite unaware of his staff. I realised that he seldom took notice of locomen either.

'Who is that man?' I asked Bert.

'Ah' said Bert, 'That's Mr Curno, the station master.'

'What's his first name?'

Bert, looking rather serious said:

'There's no first name, just Mr Curno.'

There was always a certain deference for the station master, whatever personal feelings one may have had.

There was no real need for the station master to visit the platforms on a regular basis, his foremen and inspectors were quite capable of keeping the station running smoothly.

During the night several trains called from all directions, some of these having as much as twenty minutes station time. Other than this all was quiet except for a few parcel trains, on these the porters were very busy.

The daily work commenced with the first train at 7.4am for Oxford, with fifteen services throughout the day, the last at 11.10pm. As many as thirty trains a day arrived in the down direction between 6.40am and 11pm, with eighteen in the up direction in addition to the Oxford service.

The periods of most activity were from 6.40am to about 11am, slackening off a little until 2.30pm before getting busy and easing off again at 6pm, the Oxford line being the most used in the evening. The long-distance trains had all departed by this time.

Ticket collectors were positioned at the gateways at the top of the subway stairs. When trains arrived from various directions at the same time they were hard pushed to cope with the rush, often needing assistance from a senior porter.

Throughout the night the shunting yard was kept busy preparing trains for early departure. All shunting ceased soon after 4am when two small engines came off shed

A busy Didcot station on 7 April 1932 looking west. On the centre platform the new electric and old gas lamps complement each other. Note the GWR small 'backing' signals with the two holes for identification.

Oxford County Library

Two more views of Didcot station looking west, in 1932. Work has just commenced on the up Oxford line platform. *Mowat collection*

In the lower photograph, the old loco shed is seen, with the gas works chimney in the background. *British Rail*

Didcot station staff soon after the station rebuilding in 1932.

Oxford County Library (Didcot)

The completed 1932 shed just prior to opening.

British Rail

The new shed at Didcot, 5 March 1933, (l to r) Outside framed Dean 0-6-0; 'Bulldog' 4-4-0; 0-6-0 No.2395; 2-8-0 No.2820; 0-6-0T No.1610.

VR Webster

'Dean Goods' engines and others occupy the newly built shed.

GWR Magazine

A 'Bulldog' 4-4-0 is the first loco to be tended to in the new lifting shop.

GWR Magazine

A later view of the lifting shop with an 0-6-0T under the crane. Note the forge and the communal belt-driven machinery now in use.

J Fairman

coupled together to the yard for working the 4.30am goods to Newbury and Winchester. At 5am a larger engine, either a heavy freight or mixed traffic type, left the shed for the north sidings to work to Birmingham; the crew booked off duty at their destination and after rest worked a return train the following day.

The yards more or less shut down at this time until the morning shift came on duty, their work consisted of sorting out any traffic which had collected during the night and placing it in the various sidings for unloading.

The centre yard pilot did most of this shunting which included transferring traffic to the west end sidings for the goods shed, the yards to the rear, and the provender mill. This was without doubt the most difficult yard to shunt, mainly because it was usually full with wagons and there was insufficient space to stand vehicles aside, this situation forced the shunters to shunt with long rafts of wagons attached. This in turn required the loco to pull out across the Oxford junction towards the yard, or perhaps the bay line, and sometimes even on to the up relief line. These moves quite often delayed the Oxford service, but the real problem was that the exit from the sidings was protected by a signal with a catch point; should a driver, concentrating on the shunter, fail to notice whether the signal had been replaced to danger, and move forward, there would almost certainly be a derailment. The fireman was usually held responsible by the driver to ensure that the signal was always in his favour.

During the morning the passenger pilot engine was positioned in a suitable place to await the arrival of the slip coach which would be detached from a train on the up main line at high speed. All eyes were on the Bristol train as it sped through the station at a speed of 70mph or so, then all eyes turned to watch for the slip coach gently rolling in to stop as near as possible to the top of the subway steps.

The guard would have pulled his slip lever approximately three-quarters of a mile away at the distant signal, where there was a small distant repeater particularly for his indication that it was safe to release. Without this, it could be catastrophic if the guard released and the train was stopped ahead of him by signals. I once saw this happen at Reading, fortunately without serious consequences.

The guard had very little leeway when operating the vacuum brake, there was a limit to the number of times he could apply and release the brake, moreover, each application he made reduced the effectiveness of the brake. The object was to make a positive application with considered judgement and adjust accordingly. The experienced men usually made good stops, but the inexperienced could quite easily stop short, or even overrun the platform. Should this occur the pilot engine would have to haul the slip in or perhaps have to follow it up the main line and draw it back.

On one occasion the slip failed to release for some reason, the train was stopped at Cholsey and the pilot ran the four miles to retrieve it.

The Newbury bay line, which had also been extended, served only a modicum of traffic; the first train of the day leaving at 7.38am for Southampton with only five other services throughout the day, the last of which was 6.47pm to Winchester. In addition there were only three booked freight trains during the day. However, on occasions, trains of horse-boxes went across the branch to Newbury and on to Lambourn for the racing stables.

The west end bay at the other end of the station was usually very quiet, only two stopping trains left from there for Swindon each day; 7.45am and 1.45pm. Other than that it was only used on occasions to stable an odd vehicle for unloading. In these early days of mine at Didcot, freight trains were few but by the middle of 1940 the effects of the war were really biting in. The first signs in the loco shed came when engines, which had hitherto been arriving on a regular basis for servicing, started to come in late and the arrival of most freight engines became rather haphazard. This situation led to train crews asking for relief while still *en route* to their destination, seeing no hope of arriving in time to cover their return working. Locomen are compelled to take at least twelve hours rest period before booking on duty again. This was a long standing arrangement with the BOT and the unions. This arrangement was considered by all to be an absolute necessity; the time had now come when, because of long hours on duty, it was all work and little relaxation.

In the bay platform, the 11.14 to Newbury headed by No.6164 awaits connecting passengers from the up main line train headed by 'Castle' class No.7000, 22 August 1960.
Michael Hale

A 2-6-2T runs into the east end bay bunker first from Newbury, 18 March 1960.
Joanes

CHAPTER TWO

The Better Years

Bert and I had been working together for almost a year, our turns being confined to various shunting duties intermixed with shed duties. On one of the night turns we were engaged on the coaling road, moving engines down as they were needed for coaling and then taking them away to be berthed.

At about two o'clock in the morning when our meal break was just finished the foreman came along and asked Bert:

'Do you know the road to Swindon?' – It is a must that drivers not only know the routes over which they are required to work, but that the driver must sign to show that he does.

Bert, looking puzzled, said:

'Ah, why do you ask that?'

'Well there's a train at Foxhall on the curve. The driver's asking for relief, and I've got no one else.'

'Yeah, I'll do that for you.' Bert was happy to reply. 'I'll just get my things then.'

'See you tomorrow night then Bert.' I called out.

'Hang on a minute Bert, you'll have to take your mate, that's if you don't mind.'

Bert was aware that I had no main line experience but turned to me and asked:

'Is that all right with you mate?'

Then, without a reply said:

'You'd better come along, got to do it some day.'

It was still dark when we climbed aboard the 43xx class Mogul. Bert looked at the fire and in a quiet fatherly manner, put me at ease.

'Now just try to keep the fire as it is, don't put too much coal on at a time, carry on by yourself, I'll keep an eye on you.'

The signal cleared and the engine had no difficulty getting the train of forty-five empty coal wagons away. It was all strange to me, I knew that it was twenty-four miles to Swindon but I was at a complete loss to know where I was at any time. I didn't like to keep asking Bert too much but as we rolled along steadily the fog came down, signals were difficult to see, those that Bert had been able to point out as we went along were easily seen from a distance but now I found them hard to detect even as we passed by them. The light from the open firehole lit up the fog, making it even harder to pick out the signals. The trip was

becoming an indication of what main line work was about, not all glamour.

After our successful arrival at Swindon, water was taken and I put the fire and coal right for my relief.

As we walked to the station to catch the up night sleeper back to Didcot at 5.20am, Bert praised me for my first effort, overlooking the fact that it was his guidance which made it possible, then with some solemnity, intending to keep my feet on the ground, said:

'It won't always be as easy as that. You'll find out.'

There were other small trips together, all of which were educational, but the one which stayed in my mind was when we, by chance, were booked to work one of the engines on the 4.30am goods to Newbury. This was also to be a voyage of discovery, working over a branch which I had never seen, with another engine coupled on the front, a route which went up hill and down dale, but, above all, having to control the braking of the train with the tender hand-brake.

On this first trip we were fortunate in having one of the very useful 0-6-0 23xx class engines designed by William Dean. An excellent little engine which ran freely and smoothly, steamed well, but alas had very little in the way of a cab – I can recall later trips over this branch when an overcoat or macintosh had to be worn, and the wind blew the coal off the shovel before it could reach the firehole.

Didcot has always been known for engines of second rate standard, usually locos which had been superseded by superior ones at other depots, but were still considered suitable for the work at Didcot. The better branch locos allocated to the depot were the 0-6-0 22xx class by C.B. Collett, a superb machine for the work, with a 'Castle' type cab giving plenty of cover, always master of the job. At the other end of the scale there was the dreaded 'Dukedog' type, rebuilt by Collett, numbered 90xx with the frames of the older 'Bulldog' 33xx and the boiler of the 'Duke' 3252 class, introduced in 1936 – the same year as myself. This latter engine was akin to the 3283 *Comet* except this one had wavy framing. Either way both of these were regarded as the worst engines at the shed. Any foreman in his right mind would not entertain booking two of these together on the 4.30. One coupled with a 22xx just about made it possible to get along. Bert's opinion of them was: 'They were too weak to pull the skin off a rice pudding.'

Two veterans eke out their final years as pilots at Didcot. **Above:** 2-4-0 No.3230 stands at the exit from the carriage sidings near the east end ground frame. On the footplate is 'Jim' Henry Hitchcock and 'Griff' Carter the shunter on the ground. Built at Wolverhampton, the loco worked on the Newbury line, being withdrawn in May 1922. *Author's collection*

Below: 0-6-0ST No.953 double framed and fitted with spark arrester, at Didcot, 10 June 1922. It was rebuilt as a pannier tank in April 1923 and subsequently withdrawn in September 1929. *Author's collection*

Collett 0-6-0 No.3211 waits in the carriage sidings in later years. *Real Photographs Co. Ltd.*

The fireman was not worried about that; getting the steam to do it was quite impossible, fortunately there were only these two which gave this kind of trouble.

The train usually left the yard with a full load of about five hundred tons, gently pulling past East junction box where the fireman of the second loco picked up the single-line staff, and was then responsible for changing it at each signalbox.

The pull up to the top of the Berkshire Downs was long and tedious with a gradient of 1 in 106, then upon reaching the top, the line undulated and this was where the hand-brake skills were taught and learned. In fact, the trip was very interesting, always having to be doing something.

The distance to Newbury was only eighteen miles but due to the arduous route this train was booked fifty-five minutes and, to be on the safe side, needed it. Controlling the speed of the train on the down gradients made for very slow running.

The passenger trains were always simple to handle, normally headed by a 22xx, they all steamed and ran well. There was the one odd one out which was fitted with an old ROD tender, no need for the fireman to shovel coal forward for the return, and with the extra water capacity no need either to take on water.

The most sought after trip on the branch, both for time on duty with simplicity of work, was the 7.38am to Southampton passenger. The usual engine on this service was a 33xx 4-4-0 'Bulldog' class, with the normal three or four small coaches the day's work was effortless, just one

problem, these engines slipped badly on the steep gradients.

In June 1940 I left my old mate Bert to move up into a higher link rostered to work trains only, shunting and shed work was over on a regular basis. Having considered that Bert had given me a good introduction to footplate work I felt quite confident when I joined Frank Wheeler. Once more luck was with me, Frank was also a first class mate. I mention mate because that's what footplate work was all about, working together to get the best out of an engine.

By now trains were getting almost out of hand regarding timekeeping, and within a very short time we found ourselves involved in long hours on duty, at least what we thought to be long at the time, probably twelve to fourteen hours on duty. Frank didn't like it at all, doing his utmost to avoid it. Within a space of only a few months the situation had deteriorated to the point where there was no way of avoiding excessive overtime.

It was in June of 1940 when Frank and I first became involved with long hours. The evacuation of Dunkirk by our forces had begun. To provide extra trains to transport them when they arrived back in this country some passenger trains were cancelled. In addition many freight trains were held back and those already on the road were held up for days on end. The Didcot area became completely clogged up with goods trains standing in all the loop lines, in all directions, unable to move. One instance in which Frank and I were involved highlights the seriousness of the situation at this time. We had booked on duty at 6am and were immediately given orders to relieve a train standing in the up loop at Foxhall. We duly took over, the loco was one of the huge boilered North Eastern type on loan in lieu of the Deans. At 8pm that same evening we were relieved again without having turned a wheel. During the day a number of passenger trains passed by loaded with tired and dishevelled soldiers. It was later when we found the reason.

After the statutory twelve hours rest period we returned to work and were surprised to be sent out to relieve the same loco, still having not moved. The condition of the fire and shortage of coal demanded that we take the engine to shed for a quick service before being able to work forward.

We did have one spot of trouble together, through no fault of ours we piled up a number of goods wagons in the siding at Steventon, they tipped over onto the main line causing a complete blockage.

The situation regarding slow moving goods trains never recovered, by 1941 a term had been coined, as explained below. The working fluctuated from time to time, as a result a day's work varied between eight hours for those on passenger work to anything up to twenty-four, or sometimes more than that, on the goods.

The passenger service remained constant, not only for the normal passengers but for the many service personnel now on the move.

Enemy bombing of the major towns and ports was the most serious cause of holdups. At times trains would be held up at every signal on the route to the bombed areas. The signalmen coined a phrase to explain why the trains could not move. 'We're on the block,' they would say, meaning each block signal box was unable to move a train forward. Trainmen referring to this situation said 'The block's on' indicating that it was in the lap of the gods when we could expect to see home again.

Extra men had been drafted into Didcot as a result of the terrible congestion, and by the end of 1941 the depot strength had risen from its original 45 sets to a phenomenal 110 with an equivalent number of guards. This large number of men allowed for a set to book on duty every twenty minutes throughout the day and night, solely for the purpose of relieving men who were on duty long hours.

To supervise and control the relief of trains several Didcot drivers were upgraded as supervisors. My mate, Frank, who hated overtime, took one of the appointments. I lost him after less than a year but once again had the good fortune to meet up with another gentleman driver, Harold Gasson.

The supervisors soon learned how to juggle the men to get even more out of them. They would put us on a train, say, heading towards London, and at somewhere between Didcot and Reading they would request the signalman to stop the train and ask us to change over with a train working towards Didcot. This accomplished, they then made certain that we passed Didcot with a few hours left of our duty, but with no possible hope of getting home for many hours. Trainmen went hungry for long periods, our food rations wouldn't allow for any contingencies.

The appointment of relief supervisors coincided with similar appointments within East junction signal box for the purpose of coping with this heavy surge of freight traffic.

The single line branch to Newbury was closed from August 1942 and all services suspended for the purpose of doubling the line as far as Newbury and making improvements to the southern section. Extra freight trains had been using the line for some time to alleviate the pressure on the Swindon main line. A single line was not able to carry any great volume of traffic. No indications were given as to the reason for this major work, it wasn't until the line re-opened in April 1943 that the reason became more obvious. Trains were starting to run towards Southampton on an irregular basis.

Three of the senior signalmen were upgraded to supervisory posts based within the box, their positions being filled by other men. The signalmen were now free to carry on with the work of operating the box without the need to arrange the running of trains, this was now being done for them, the supervisor sorted out the traffic priorities.

A notice was issued to all signal boxes in the area as follows:

GREAT WESTERN RAILWAY
DIVISIONAL SUPERINTENDENT'S OFFICE PADDINGTON, LONDON, 4 JUNE 1942
REGULATION OF TRAINS – DIDCOT EAST JUNCTION
TO COMMENCE, MONDAY 8 JUNE 1942
The regulation of all trains, i.e. passenger, parcels, freight, military, Naval and RAF Specials, empty stock, etc., on the up and down lines in the area bounded by Goring, Milton, Radley, and Compton will be vested in three special class relief signalmen employed at Didcot East junction for train regulation purposes. The closest co-operation must be maintained by these men with the station masters, Reading Control, signalmen and relief supervisors in order that the maximum beneficial results in train working may be obtained by this co-ordination of movements in the area.
The relief signalman must confer with the station master and/or inspectors whenever there is congestion at the station likely to cause undue delay.

ADVICE OF TRAIN RUNNING
READING WEST JUNCTION:
To advise Didcot East junction the passing times of all down trains.
OXFORD SOUTH:
To advise Didcot East junction the passing times of all up trains.
COMPTON:
To advise Didcot East junction of all up trains.
HIGHWORTH JUNCTION:
To advise Didcot Foxhall junction and Didcot East junction the passing times of all up trains.
Foxhall junction to transmit the information in respect of Oxford line trains to Didcot North junction.

Used on the Newbury line, 'Duke' class No.3267 *Cornishman* stands in Didcot shed in the early 1930s. It was withdrawn in October 1936.   *Real Photographs*

Ex MSWJ 2-4-0 No.1335, when stationed at Didcot, was used mainly on the Newbury line and Lambourn branch. It is seen here in the 1930s, finally leaving Didcot in 1938.   *P Earl*

No.2935 *Caynham Court* stands in Didcot west end bay c.1933. This loco was fitted with Poppet valve gear in May 1931. In the author's time at Didcot during the war years, the loco was regularly employed working a stopping train from Swindon to Didcot and returning with the 2.35pm stopper. It was withdrawn from service in December 1948.

Brian Davis collection

Instructions of a similar nature were issued to all signal boxes which had any bearing on the regulation of trains at Didcot, including the yard and the ordnance depot when trains were ready to leave.

From 1941 two regular trains departed the depot each day; one at 11.15am for Hanwell Bridge sidings near Southall, and one at 11.30pm for Birmingham. Other special trains worked out as required and various rafts of wagons were brought out to the yard by one of the depot pilot engines.

The reason for doubling the Newbury branch had been the subject of much conjecture. Now it had become obvious that the line was to be one of the main routes to carry supplies for the re-entry into Europe by our forces.

The authority for doubling the branch was given in 1942 with an estimated cost to the Ministry of Transport of £247,850.

Work commenced 4 August 1942 when the line was closed to all traffic and re-opened when the work was completed in April 1943.

Inspection of the work was ordered 26 June 1943 to be carried out by Col. R.J. Walker and C.A. Langley. Once again there was an unusual lapse before the line was inspected, in fact, six years. The inspection was finally completed on 18 March 1949. The inspectors made a somewhat bland statement when they commented 'the work was executed at high speed', considering the length of their own delay.

The main remarks on the line included:

The single line signalling was altered to conform with the standard GWR signalling practice (double line) with three position block instruments installed.... Block working was operated between all stations with an additional section box at Hampstead Norris and intermediate electrically operated signals (with Distant) at Churn.

The report concluded:

Traffic never reached the anticipated intensity and at the present time it is light. The line is however of strategic importance in connection with Military movements to the Southampton and Portsmouth area. This last comment should have been in the past tense.

This report makes a mockery of the inspection, not only was it carried out four years after the end of the war, when the reason for its use was now over, but it also failed to recognise the amount of traffic that used the line for military purposes and the further benefit in easing the congestion between Didcot and Swindon.

Working across the branch took on a new dimension, those little old fashioned engines which fitted in so well with the country line were quite inadequate to haul the heavier trains now running. The track had been strengthened some years ago to allow larger engines to work over it, but that, even then, only went as far as allowing the 2-6-0 43xx Mogul over the line. With the doubling, the track was again strengthened to permit the larger 2-8-0 28xx, a loco which was more than powerful enough to take the equivalent load of forty-five ten-ton loaded wagons, the maximum load for the line and gradients. Although I say it was more than powerful enough, the tensile strength of the couplings dictated the load on a bank.

Harold and I took the first train down to Southampton with a 28xx. There were several turntables in the dockyard sidings but they were far too small for any of the locos which worked in. Turning was normally done by reversing on one of the many triangles, but these were also too tight in the radius to allow the 28xx to run round without doing some damage, such as spreading the track or, even worse, becoming derailed. There was insufficient play in the eight coupled wheel arrangement for free movement within the axlebox horn plates.

We couldn't work all the way back tender first so Harold suggested that we go back to Eastleigh loco to turn. That suggestion was met with a most positive rebuff from the army officer who had charge of the docks and had a principle that engines must not leave the docks without taking a train out. Under no circumstances would he trust us to return, and had no intention of giving way.

The outcome was that a dock pilotman took us to several locations to assess the merits of the various triangles, moving gently with an awful squealing of flanges as they bit in and juddered their precarious way round the tight curves. Eventually a triangle was found which seemed to be just about safe, providing the speed did not exceed 5mph.

Many long hours were wasted by waiting for trains to be unloaded before we could return. Many of these trips we worked together, none ever being less than fourteen hours on duty. This was, I suppose, my small contribution to the war effort.

While in the thick of this I moved up again to what was known as the goods link. Harold had always insisted that I took a share of the driving, it was great of him to give me such a good insight while he was there to guide me. My new mate and I didn't get off to such a good start, I didn't like the way he worked the engine hard, which meant that reflected upon my work. The manual side wasn't troubling me but when it came to the point of failing to get steam because he was using it faster than I could make it, and then blaming me, tension rose. It was a long time before I came to terms with the situation.

The higher link working took us to further distances and directions. We now worked via the branch line to Westbury also the opposite direction, via Oxford to Worcester. Either way the work was more tedious for me. The driver knew the routes very well and handled the trains well but unfortunately not the engine. To make matters worse the engines were not getting the attention they should and were invariably poor steamers. Coal was often poor quality so with the combination of these things and some stiff gradients on these routes I had the ignominy of having to come to a stand on several occasions on gradients to, what we used to say, 'have a blow-up'. The last straw was when we were slogging up Honeybourne bank with Worcester men on a banker at the rear. We were on one of the old ROD engines left over from the previous war, they would plod along for hours with little steam, they normally had to, never gave anything away. Now add this to my previously mentioned problems and it was quite understandable when we gradually puffed ourselves to a stop long before the top of the bank was reached.

On the Westbury road things were much the same, but I was not alone here, most firemen could boast that they had been forced to stop for steam at Bedwyn, half way up the bank to Savernake.

Another unusual episode of the war years cropped up at this time. Coal supplies to London had been so interfered with due to the bombing that stocks became desperately low. To overcome this and get supplies built up again, several special trains ran on Sundays for a number of weeks. Each train consisted of one hundred ten-ton wagons of coal, the total weight of the train amounting to about 1,500 tons. A 28xx was at the head and from the starting point at Severn Tunnel junction, a banker was at the rear to Swindon. Here the crew were relieved, either by Swindon or Didcot men. I had the experience on one occasion only, but quite frankly, it didn't seem any different to an ordinary train of sixty wagons. The line dropped very steadily towards London and with a little care approaching signals, there was very little problem.

By comparison to all this aggravation and exceptionally long hours it was quite a relief and pleasure to be booked to work a passenger train. This only happened when I was due for a spare turn, for the purpose of covering a vacant duty. It was a pleasure to be able to know that at a certain time, the day's work was over. Some of the more memorable services were: 7.38am Southampton; 7.4am Banbury; 7.45am Swindon; 1.45pm Swindon, but this one should have been avoided if possible, invariably had a 32xx class on it, trouble all the way. The 3.45pm to Paddington was also a nice turn to work, except that by the time of departure home at 8.10pm the enemy was always around, somewhere in the city bombs were falling, anti-aircraft guns were firing, shrapnel fell around at times. It was a relief to get away but it seems we were never in any real danger, maximum speed until outside the danger area was limited to 15mph.

Special troop trains were also a diversion from the everyday freight train crawl. As the time grew nearer to a landing on the continent troops were moved to strategic positions along the coast. My driver, in common with the other senior men, had a greater knowledge of routes and therefore was called upon to work some of these trains. One train which springs to mind was of ten coaches worked from Oxford via Reading to Yeovil with a 43xx and a tender full with coke instead of coal, then return to Banbury.

Arriving from the Oxford direction 2-8-0 No.3820 gently hauls a southbound freight over Didcot North junction signalled into No.1 yard reception road.

Rodney Lissenden

Many of these trains were moving American troops from their inland camps to areas for embarkation. By the time the men were moved practically all the stores and equipment were in place. For some considerable time now the movements towards the coast had been carried out without interference from enemy planes. Stores still left the ordnance depot on a regular basis, including many additional trains to the various army depots about the country.

When I arrived at Didcot it was to fill a normal vacancy for promotion. There wasn't any scramble to find lodgings and I was very fortunate to be able to live with a railway family. Later, when the influx of men arrived, they had difficulty finding accommodation. Eventually the railway in their wisdom provided a number of sleeping coaches and parked them at the rear of the loco shed, outside the end of two, three and four roads. Drivers and firemen arrived from all parts of the GWR, most of whom were comparatively inexperienced.

At first this seemed to be the answer to the accommodation problem, the men were happy to have somewhere to live. But soon the difficulties manifested themselves. There were severe problems for the men in providing food for themselves, but perhaps worse was the washing facilities which comprised only of the wash hand basins at the ends of the coaches and those in the men's toilets in the shed.

Sleeping and living two to a compartment with nowhere to dry any wet clothing and no clothes washing arrangements, having no privacy, the situation became intolerable.

Eventually the problem was overcome when the Ministry of Works sanctioned the building of a hostel at the bottom of Station Road to accommodate these men. It was opened on 3 May 1944, much to the delight of the men in the coaches. There were a hundred individual rooms with reading and rest rooms. Best of all they had a canteen and baths. The canteen was opened to all railwaymen, as were several at different locations. The men who hitherto had suffered such long hours without food were now able to stave off the pangs of hunger. It wasn't Ritz food but it tasted just as good to us.

In the small hours of the morning of 6 June 1944 I was trundling along the up relief line towards Reading on a Collett 22xx with a freight train, plagued with the usual signal to signal stops. Beyond Goring we came to a stop at the intermediate block signal and waited for some time. While waiting to move on there came a heavy rumbling in the sky, a sound I had not heard before. Watching the sky I eventually noticed red and green flares floating in the sky in pairs, as one pair went out others lit up. The noise became louder and the number of flares increased. Dawn was about to break and as it did the light revealed hundreds of American bombers getting into formation, they appeared to be forming into square boxes of one hundred. There were so many that all the planes could not be seen together until they flew off in a south-easterly direction.

It was several hours before we moved on to Pangbourne to find that D-Day had begun. There was a sense of freedom knowing that the enemy would be too preoccupied in his own defence to bother us any more.

Immediately the push was on, there was an upsurge in trains to Southampton to maintain supplies. The saddest job of all was being asked to take an ambulance train away somewhere to the north. We had arrived in the docks with a string of American locomotives for shipment to France, arriving with plenty of time for the return working. When the train was due to leave, the medical officer came to the driver and asked if he could possibly run slowly as there were seriously wounded men on board. We worked as far as Banbury, having a priority non-stop run all the way. This train was one of two which were based in the carriage sidings at Reading. Two other trains stood at Newbury, worked by men from the North Eastern Railway who were able to continue through to destination without delay.

As the movement of government stores gradually diminished, things in general slowed down, the excessive hours on duty became less frequent, food rationing to railwaymen had increased a little, it was now, not if the war would end, but when?

In retrospect it was difficult to imagine how quiet Didcot had been when I first arrived and how the work multiplied to such a degree, the quiet shed where one driver and mate could cope, now had three. The fire-droppers had also increased to three and the coalman had an assistant. The coal stage which was normally supplied once a day required at least two supplies and often three. The ash pit where the fires were cleared out had a fairly large shed built to cover the chance of enemy planes seeing the hot ashes being thrown out but, as it transpires, was never needed.

The station had never seen such numbers of passengers and parcels, the platforms at times were a jumble of goods in transit. Service personnel filled the trains travelling to and from leave. These were so numerous at times that the army requested special furlough trains.

At midnight on 12 May 1945 the war in Europe finally came to an end, the greatly increased activity which Didcot had become involved in ended rather more quickly than it had built up. On 12 September victory over Japan was announced.

The additional men who had been drafted to augment the train crews were soon repatriated to their own depots. Many of these men remained unknown, that is, they were so often in the background, if not out working the long hours, never surfacing long enough to become known.

The role of Didcot was far more serious and satisfying than could ever have been envisaged when Brunel first planned it.

The ordnance depot now had no need to handle the vast amount of stores and was gradually run down. Slowly, over twenty years, the depot was emptied of its stock, the remaining items now required were transferred to a depot at Bicester. During September 1964 the ordnance depot closed for good.

The railway hostel at Didcot opened to accommodate train crews during the war.

British Rail

I had arrived at Didcot to fill a vacancy and therefore was not sent away as the others were. It was January 1945 when I left to return home by special application.

Soon after the war ended there was another revolution in rail travel. The war weary country was looking for some means of escape, taking to the rails in great numbers for holidays at the seaside for the first time in six years.

At the recognised holiday periods, particularly August, all trains to seaside resorts were crammed, many extra trains were laid on. Some trains, particularly from the north were run in two or even three parts. Everything, including Didcot, was settling down to some sort of normality.

In the early 1950s the motor car became more available to people in general. This newly found freedom of the open road, together with its convenience, slowly drew large numbers of passengers away from the railways. Local services, particularly branch lines, suffered by having services curtailed. The fall in passenger travel crept through the system, matched only by the reduction in parcel and freight traffic. Road transport was taking its toll.

The railway junction at Didcot became a shadow of its wartime eminence. It had proved the wisdom of Brunel in siting the junction at this point, but what was the reason behind this decision?

By looking back we can get a picture of what was in the mind of this 'engineering Knight-errant'.

CHAPTER THREE

Dudcote and the Railway

Dudcote, as it was once known, was a little village nestling under the northern rim of the Berkshire Downs. Its population at the beginning of the nineteenth century is recorded as being 181. In the next sixty years or so it increased at the rate of approximately one a year to reach about 251 by the middle of the century.

Didcot had very little recognition from any source. *Kelly's Directory* of 1847 quotes Didcott as being five miles from Abingdon, with no comment regarding its status. William Robert Baker is identified as being Lord of The Manor, and the Church living of £457 being held by the Revd Joseph Hodgkinson. Eight farmers are also named together with a grocer and draper, school master, parish clerk and the landlords of two public houses. Also noted was that mail was received from Abingdon.

In 1851 *Billing's Directory* gave the distance as being six to six and a half miles to Abingdon, quoted as being the nearest market town; one of a triangle of three formed with Wallingford to the east and Wantage to the west. The community has been described in various directories as either a village, or as a parish, but perhaps the most apt is that given in 1863 in *Cassey's Directory*, which referred to 'a village and a parish'. In this context the village would be that of Old Didcot as it is now referred to. The mail was now delivered from Wallingford.

At the later date of 1887 *Kelly's Directory* now agrees that the distance to Abingdon is six and a half miles, with a Didcot population of 373. The living has now been taken over by the Revd John A. Ashworth MA. Colonel Lord Wantage VC KBE has now taken over as Lord of The Manor. At this time Christopher Evans was the station master with John Adams the manager of the provender stores. George Drew managed the *Junction Hotel* and also had the contract for the railway refreshment rooms. The *Queen's Arms* in the Old Village was in the hands of William Williams. Two coal merchants were now in business, one, E.S. Copeland, being registered at the railway station. Various small tradesmen are listed and eight local tenant farmers.

This is the site of the original village with its Church of All Saints as the focal point. A church is known to have stood on this site as early as the ninth or tenth century and at some time replaced and further enlarged. The village has a wealth of old houses, the most historic of which is known as *White Cottage*, the history of which is believed to go back almost to medieval times. There are many old timbered houses and farm buildings still in use today.

Yet there still remains the doubt regarding the origin of the name. References can be found in several directories of the mid-nineteenth century with varying spellings of the name, also maps drawn by the most eminent cartographers of the time are also at odds. From a list of maps and other sources the following names are identified:

Maps of Berkshire

Christopher Saxton,	1579	Didcott
William Kipp,	1607	Didcote
John Speed,	1611	Dudcot
John Blaue,	1645	Dudcot
R Morden,	1695	Dutcott
John Cary	1801	Didcott
James Whittle,	1806	Didcott
A. Fullerton	1843	Didcott

From Letters and Other Sources

Mr Humbleton,	1838	Didcot
I.K. Brunel,	1839/40	Dudcot
Revd R. Gilbert,	1840	Didcote
" " "	1841	Didcott
Ordnance Survey,	1874	Dudcote

From these recorded various spellings and casual comments it must be deduced that the village was very little known prior to the advent of the railway. It also seems strange that the 1874 Ordnance Survey still has the name Dudcote thirty years after the Great Western Railway had virtually settled the issue, by naming the station Didcot junction.

Even so, Mr Humbleton, a local solicitor, seems to be the first to mention the present spelling in one of his letters to the Oxford colleges when they squabbled over the purchase of a client's land. Further to this an unsigned letter dated 28 June 1800 contains yet another variation of the spelling: '...at this time the parish church living at Dudecote was £335 per annum.'

The generally accepted belief for the name Dudcote derives from Ralph de Dudcote, the Abbot of nearby Dorchester Abbey, c1292. This theory is born out by the finding of an effigy in the churchyard of All Saints Church. The effigy was accidentally discovered by workmen, lying

A typical scene at Old Didcot. The *White Cottage* on the right is recorded as being the oldest in Didcot   *Mrs Iris Moon*

In the centre of Old Didcot with the school gates on the right and the only village shop with its bay window. *Author's collection*

face downwards with its flat surface uppermost, forming what appeared to be an unusually large flagstone which was used as part of the churchyard path.

This was a community almost unknown outside of its own boundaries, the roads were poor, only suitable for farm carts. The turnpike road from Wallingford to Wantage passed close by, but very few, if any, ventured down the narrow lane to do business with the village. A road did exist which came in from the Oxford direction via Abingdon and Appleford to enter Dudcote from the north-east, turning towards the village in a westerly direction but again with very little prospect of bringing in any business. As such, trade was almost non-existent, there seems to have been only one small general store, the farm workers having a subsidy of farm produce occasionally as part of their wages.

No doubt there were a few local tradesmen in the way of blacksmiths, farriers and harness-makers for the only, and most important, means of transport. Builders, thatchers, carpenters and perhaps a bootmaker could be found with the possibility of a travelling tinker plying his trade.

The major portion of the land in the area was owned by either Lord Wantage or the Church under the umbrella of the Oxford colleges. These influential people determined the use of the land and all who lived from it.

There was little for the traveller and no need for visitors. The only travellers who passed this way on the turnpike road were stopped at a toll gate to pay taxes to his Lordship. In later years there was a public house on the outskirts of the village named the *Queen's Arms* which still exists in almost the same form today. Whatever its age, in the beginning it would have been the only means of pleasure in the village. The only other means of community spirit was the accepted regular Sunday service.

This situation was allowed to continue and certainly would have done so for many years had it not been for the development of the railways. When the railways came to the country no one could have foreseen the dramatic changes which took place in hundreds of towns and villages. One can be almost certain that the purpose of building the railways was solely for the benefit of company shareholders with the object in mind of increasing wealth. The population of the country in general were not considered; how it affected them and their wellbeing was of little importance. Some communities were left isolated and at the same time others were to gain a great advantage. Dudcote was a little different, in that it neither stood still nor prospered in the same way as others, but developed in its own distinct way.

The credit for this and the surrounding areas has always been given to the GWR. Quite rightly so, because it finally brought the railway to the area; but there were other factors which played a large part, indeed the GWR took up the options which others had rejected for one reason or another. Although there had been three earlier abortive schemes for a railway to be run from Bristol to London, it was not until the autumn of 1832 that four Bristol merchants – Thomas Guppy, John Harford, George Jones and William Tothill – formed themselves into a committee with the aim of establishing The Bristol Railway, and on 21 January 1833 they held their first full meeting.

On 7 March Isambard Kingdom Brunel was appointed Engineer. His first task was to survey the two routes previously planned by others – one by John McAdam who was experienced in building turnpike roads. Within a few weeks he had produced a plan for a railroad from Bristol via Wootton Bassett, through the Vale of the White Horse in Wiltshire to Wantage and on to Wallingford, then to follow the River Thames to Reading and then by one of two routes to London. The other route surveyed by two gentlemen, Brunton and Price, followed a similar route to Bathampton, then turned away to Trowbridge and near to Devizes before entering the rather hilly country through the Pewsey Vale to Hungerford, Newbury and Reading. The gradient of 1 in 53 on the GWR line up to Devizes indicates how severe the terrain was.

The Bristol and London committees met in London on 22 August 1833. Brunel was confirmed as Engineer by the London Committee on 27 August; much to his pleasure, knowing that he had at this time made very good friends with the newly appointed secretary, Charles Saunders, who was to be his constant ally. Brunel was delighted with his appointment to what he considered to be the greatest engineering project of the time. The imposing title 'Great Western Railway' suggested by his father, Marc, spurred his imagination more than the originally suggested 'Grand'. That night Isambard made an entry in his diary – **GWR** – in bold letters.

Isambard, although being delighted with his appointment, was more than a little displeased at having William Townsend working with him on an even footing, to carry out the surveying. Townsend had only limited experience in building a railway, the extent of which was a ten-mile coal tramway. Even then, it was, at this stage, more than Brunel himself. Brunel's ambition was to be the sole Engineer in charge, to take the credit for what he deemed to be the greatest railway to date. He was greatly concerned and wrote 'How am I to get on with him tied to my neck.'

The route which Brunel finally proposed left Bristol and then via Bath, Chippenham, Swindon, then in an almost straight and level line through the Vale of The White Horse and on through the Thames valley to Reading and London. By following the levels of the rivers he hoped to keep the cost of construction to a minimum.

On 30 July Brunel explained his proposals – the line would be 116 miles long and would cost, complete with stations and 38 locos, £2½m. This was to be nearly a triple underestimate on Brunel's part. The prospect of saving on locomotive power with the level line appealed to him very much; it was also very much appreciated over the years by locomotivemen, myself included.

These proposals were put forward in July of that year

The *Wheatsheaf* public house along the Wantage Road in the latter part of the nineteenth century.   *Author's collection*

A later picture of Old Didcot showing the *Queens Arms* public house on the right and the *White Cottage* in the centre.

Author's collection

and at the Parliamentary session, in giving his evidence for the main reasons for the proposed route, he said:

The general inclination of the line was particularly favourable since for more than 100 miles from London to Wootton Bassett in Wiltshire it is almost completely level. Even the excavations and banks required virtually correspond in quantity and amount to only about 8,000,000 cubic yards in the whole 116 miles.

At the first joint meeting of the Bristol and London Committees on 19 August 1833 the title 'Great Western Railway' was officially adopted. It was then stated that the cost of the line was estimated to be £1,805,330 for the construction of the line throughout, and that construction would take up to four to five years.

The maps presented at this meeting were known to have had 'probable branch lines on them' including one from Dudcote to Oxford. The first plans to be drawn up routed the line close to Abingdon and also Wallingford. These plans were soon abandoned because of very strong objections from the landowners of Abingdon, backed very firmly by the Oxford colleges. A plan similar to this did reach the Parliamentary stage only to be rejected for an amendment to be added to the effect that 'the line must take another route away from that town.' It was most likely then that the knowledge of this refusal prompted Brunel to adopt the more straightforward line avoiding both Abingdon and Wallingford, going as it does through Dudcote, suggesting as he did 'that branch lines could be added at a later date.' The main line, as now planned, would follow the Thames for most of the way to London.

Several sites for a terminal in London had been considered; one which appealed to him was to run into Euston on the London & Birmingham Railway's line, joining in the region of the present Queen's Park station. This plan had to be dropped and replaced by an extension into Paddington.

Brunel and his staff had been extremely busy with the details of this more improved project, but at the same time it was more definite. In an extract from an undated letter which he wrote to John Hammond, his assistant, he mentioned, 'it is harder work than I like, I am rarely under twenty hours a day at it.'

Further points in favour of a railway were put at the Parliamentary session:

...that it multiply the number of travellers, improve the conveyance of goods, encourage manufacturers, diffuse the advantage of the town over the country intersected by the railway, improve the supply of materials to the metropolis and extend the market for agricultural produce, give employment to the labouring classes, both during the construction and by its subsequent effects, and increase the value of the property in the neighbourhood.

The Thames Commissioners were expected to lose most to this new form of transport. It was they who had control of the important waterway connecting the Kennet & Avon canal to London. They agreed that:

...it is unanimously resolved that the general committee be instructed and empowered to take all such steps as they shall deem advisable for effectively opposing the progress of this useless and mischievous project.

For two years the two most influential newspapers of Reading took opposite sides in the controversy, causing public response to be over-cautious, leaving many shares unsold. The GWR, bitter at the fact that half their shares had not yet been sold, and thus being unable to raise the required capital, were now unable to put their case to Parliament.

The directors decided on an alternative plan. In what can only be described as desperation, they conceived a plan to build from Reading to London and at the same time also, to build from Bristol to Bath, no doubt to gain a foothold with the prospect of completing the whole line at a later and more favourable date. This ploy was again forestalled by the landowners who each in turn denied having agreed to sell their land in the first place. Various speakers rose at a meeting held in December of 1833 dealing with the effects on local agriculture and vested interests, one of whom added:

...to say nothing of the destruction of the land, the asseverence of enclosures, the inundation of foreign labourers, and the increased poor rate.

Lord Palmer, the MP for Berkshire, who resided on the outskirts of Reading, tried to give some support to the railway. Speaking at a public meeting in Reading he said:

...the line would destroy some of my farms and divide my estate, but I feel that if the projectors could make out a case, then private feeling must make way for good.

However, at the end of the meeting the landowners agreed:

...it would be injurious to their interest, repugnant to their feelings, and that no case for the public utility had been made to justify such an uncalled for encroachment on the rights of private property.

The opposition had, it is plain to see, fought hard and furious to prevent the GWR from succeeding with its plans.

The controversy continued for several more months with the local newspapers taking sides. Letters from readers were printed throughout the winter, some of which severely criticised the Thames Commissioners for what they saw as an unnecessary stand. One such letter printed in the *Reading Mercury*, which favoured the railway, included a strong attack on Mr Payne, the opponents' secretary:

Mr Payne is driven to his wits end to make out a case to justify his pernicious opposition to the projected railway. There must be as much public utility in a railway as in a turnpike road or a canal or a river made navigable.... The proposed line is fraught with almost incalculable good to the nation, and particularly along the line of its operation by bringing in an immense power of capital and industry into mutual co-operation...

These arguments were countered by the opposition newspaper, the *Reading Chronicle*, entreating everyone to be cautious, pointing out that:

...the scheme is now only to get power to make two railways from Bristol to Bath and from Reading to London... and if the company should neglect to complete from Reading to Bath, what a deception the public will be drawn into...

Very serious disagreements were also raised in the area of Slough, mainly from the Provost of Eton College. He felt that the railway would be injurious to the school. The main worry of the Provost of Eton was that the GWR would put the London brothels within easy reach of the aristocratic schoolboys. As to the trades people of Windsor who, he claimed, relied upon the school for their support, they should consider the prosperity of the college and therefore their own.

One of the more worthwhile reasons for building a railway was often overlooked. It was the fact that during the hard winter months the Thames often froze over making navigation impossible, or storms wrecked the barges. In addition the summer droughts lowered the level of the river, leaving barges stranded for weeks on end. When such circumstances occurred the freight had to be transferred to road vehicles. The carriers took advantage of the situation, increasing the charges for the service, other than that, the perishable goods were lost altogether.

By the end of February 140 burgesses had signed a petition requesting the Mayor of Reading to call a meeting and ask the Great Western Railway to send a representative to give more information. As a result a meeting was called in March 1834, to be addressed by Charles Saunders, secretary to the company. Among other things he said:

The situation of Reading has rendered it a very favourable resort and the influx of strangers cannot but be increased if the town is brought within one and a half to two hours of London, instead of the present four and a half to five hours... will it be of no advantage to the town to see those beautiful mansions – many of which are now untenanted – filled, as they will be, if we can ensure a mode of conveyance expeditious, secure, without fatigue, and cheap.

Four days later the Great Western Railway Company bill was introduced to the House of Commons. The Mayor and burgesses of Reading were represented by their MP, Charles Russell, other petitions from the opposition were also presented, including that of the local landowners of Berkshire. The bill was well supported in the Commons but failed in the Lords.

The GWR now realised that public opinion was turning in its favour and prepared another more beneficial bill for the next session and invited subscriptions for a further 10,000 shares. The bill was passed by the end of August and by early September it received the Royal Assent. The Great Western Railway was born.

The *Reading Chronicle*, which had always supported the opposition, rather ingratiously bowed out with a report in their newspaper on 5 September:

The bill for carrying the measure into effect, having passed both houses of Parliament, received the Royal Assent on Monday last... we have not heard yet what decision has been made by the inhabitants of the towns on the high road between Reading and Bristol, but we should advise them of the great change which the railway will effect in their trade.

The railway and its opponents had fought a bitter battle but throughout neither side were showing any consideration for the population in general. The railway was seen by them only as it affected their trade and prosperity. The arguments were put merely as a sham. No consideration was given to the people living directly in the areas which the railway impinged upon, nor even to the sometimes greater effect to those outside its influence. To this end some towns would be in a position to expand and develop whilst others – more remote – would languish.

Opposition had prevailed throughout the length of the proposed line but none so fierce as at the London end. The magnitude of the venture was fraught with opposition, possibly because it was a far greater and more ambitious project than any to date.

Although the railways of the north had by this time shown that success was possible, who could have foreseen what the ultimate outcome would be. There can be little doubt that the subsequent prosperity of towns such as Reading can only be attributed largely to the arrival of the Great Western Railway.

Such was the situation when the railway was built at Dudcote during 1840. The line was opened 1 June 1840 to Steventon by-passing Dudcote, practically running through its back garden as it were, not having any immediate effect on the local population. After the initial interest they hardly noticed and were certainly not noticed themselves. During the period of construction the local people would no doubt have felt they were overburdened with the influx of workmen seeking lodgings, at the same time pleased to be able to supplement their income a little. Soon this was to be almost forgotten, that is, until Didcot had its own station, four years later.

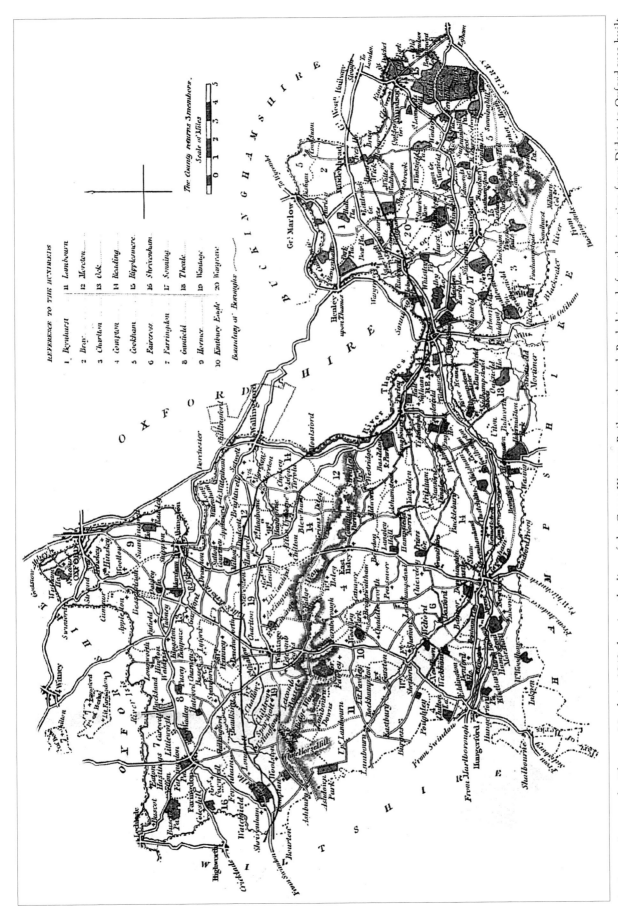

An interesting map by Thomas Moule in 1843 showing the line of the Great Western Railway through Berkshire, before the junction from Didcot to Oxford was built. Note the spelling as Dudcott even though the Ordnance Survey at this time still called it Dudcote. The name was settled the following year when the new station was named Didcot Junction.

CHAPTER FOUR

Building the Railway

Directly the Royal Assent was given the Great Western Railway soon got under way. The plans which were once formulated to build from London to Reading and also from Bristol to Bath were now put into immediate operation with no further need to survey. These sections were in the most advanced stages of readiness and seemed to be the most expeditious means of achieving an early start.

Sections were completed in stages and opened as soon as they were ready. The first section from Paddington (old station) to Maidenhead (old station, now Taplow) was opened in June 1838; Maidenhead to Twyford in December 1839; and Twyford to Reading in March 1840. This represented a rate of about twelve miles a year. In the official history of the GWR, E.T. MacDermot wrote:

The contracts for the line as far as Didcot were let early in 1838, ...west of Didcot, as far as Uffington, the contracts were let in March, and this was proceeding rapidly.

The letting for contracts as far as Didcot and separately beyond suggests that Didcot was a focal point in the minds of the company and could point to the fact that there were serious thoughts of creating the Oxford junction there, as was envisaged in the reference to 'a probable branch to Oxford.' Brunel also referred to *Dudcot* as being an engineering limit in his letter to the Railway Board in 1840, in which he wrote:

Beyond Reading and up to Dudcot, a distance of seventeen and a half miles, the ballasting is complete with the exception of two short lengths, together about two and a half miles. The difficulty of procuring ballast for this part has been great, the ground purchased for this purpose being under water, and it being necessary to dredge the river in order to obtain gravel.

The laying of the rails is in a forward state, a single line being laid for fifteen miles, upon which the materials for the second line are being carried and distributed to all parts so that work will proceed rapidly. Beyond Dudcot great exertions have been made to complete the line for an opening to a point near Farrington simultaneously with the opening to Reading, the opening may be calculated June or the beginning of July.

The twenty and a half miles from Reading to Steventon

with intermediate stations at Pangbourne, Goring and Wallingford Road (now repositioned and named Cholsey), were opened to the public in June 1840.

Steventon, of course, meant 'Steventon for Oxford', ten miles away on the turnpike road. Passengers for Oxford were required to suffer the remainder of their journey by road in bumpy horse-drawn carriages, but even then they were probably happy about the overall reduction in the travelling time.

Brunel's decision to terminate the line at Steventon where the turnpike road crossed was a shrewd move favouring the travellers to Oxford. The objections raised by both the residents of Abingdon and the Oxford colleges had forced this move upon the railway, but at the same time, was it a ploy on the part of Brunel to ultimately achieve his ambition to drive through to the north with Oxford as his first step? By giving a service to those wishing to use the railway, and thereby proving the value of the railway above that of road travel, and at the same time allowing them to suffer the last ten miles in comparative discomfort, would surely have converted them to a preference for a through line to Oxford. If influential men used this new means of travel, they in turn would certainly bring pressure to bear on those in opposition. Whatever devious intentions were employed the preference to rail travel was implanted.

Following the opening of the line as far as Steventon some interesting comments were printed in the *Wallingford News*, 6 June 1840:

Opening at Cholsey of line from Steventon to Reading on Monday last. Journey from London to station (Steventon) in two hours ten minutes, incredible time. Thousands of spectators flowed to Steventon, morning quiet, village overwhelmed, in afternoon first train arrived hauled by locomotive The Leopard. *Many people, just for curiosity sake, went to London and back.*

The same newspaper also printed an assurance that a coach service would still run from London, and coaches would come also from as far away as Birmingham.

There were advertisements by various operators providing a service to either Steventon or Cholsey daily. Costain & Waddle were to run coaches from Oxford to Steventon and also to Moulsford (Wallingford Road station)

An official picture of Steventon in April 1951 when the station and yard had become quite deserted. It is difficult to believe this quiet country station was, albeit briefly, the centre of Great Western government. The board met in the large house in the centre of the picture.

British Rail

to meet every train up and down – eight trains a day.

An interesting comment appeared in the same newspaper on 12 September 1840:

In 1813 it took thirty hours from Cheltenham to London sleeping one night at Oxford; in 1840 the journey is done by rail in six.

During the building of the railway there was a great influx of labour into the area. The large number of Irish navvies employed found difficulty in getting lodgings, the small village of Dudcote was swamped with men searching for accommodation and in most cases the best they could do was to settle for a bed for the night and obtain food elsewhere. There were no local inns to accommodate them and those unable to settle in the village had the additional effort of walking to other nearby villages. However, this inconvenience to the villagers lasted for only a few months because, as Brunel said, 'the work in the area was of a slight nature and was proceeding well.' Trains continued to stop at Steventon for the convenience of Oxford passengers for another four years, prompting the Commissioners to regard the station with first class status.

Perhaps for Dudcote it was not quite the same as before, the novelty of the railway and trains passing by at speed would have changed their outlook a little. On 1 June 1840, the day of the opening, it seemed that everyone turned out to see the passing of the first train, from the excellent vantage point along the embankment between the station and the new Foxhall Road bridge, and the even better position on the bridge itself for those who dared. They watched in awe and a certain amount of trepidation as the train passed by at about 30mph drawn by the locomotive the *Leopard*, one of the 'Firefly' class with its gleaming brasswork and tall chimney throwing out steam and smoke. The locomotive was one of several of its type with a 2-2-2 wheel arrangement, the single driving wheels of 7ft made the loco very impressive with 4ft carrying wheels each side. The boiler was horizontal with a square upright firebox and had no protection for the driver and fireman, they stood on a small footplate with only a handrail to keep them from falling off. The locomotive was built in 1840 by Sharp, Roberts & Company of Manchester with two cylinders 18in stroke by 15in bore and a boiler pressure of 50 psi. The tender was fitted with a covered seat for the train guard to sit facing the train to see that it was following correctly.

It must be considered then, that it was more by chance than design that Dudcote had a railway so near. Had Abingdon not rejected it so forcibly the line would have been laid on a route which gave most benefit to the three market towns of Abingdon, Wantage and Wallingford. These three towns were all of similar status, each with its market square and the usual tradesmen. Had the line followed this route, Dudcote would have been isolated.

The final decision to keep the line as straight and as level as possible drew it away from Wantage by about two miles, almost three from Wallingford, and Abingdon was about two and a half miles from the Oxford main line when it was eventually opened. Ultimately all three were connected to the main line of the GWR by single line branches, but without the main line on their path they were not able to prosper in the same way as did towns such as Reading, and so basically remained the same small market towns which they had always been.

The Board of Directors adopted a report in October 1841 that the separate London and Bristol Committees were to be abolished and Traffic and General Committees appointed. These two committees to meet weekly. All meetings of the board and committees to be held at Steventon, 'if the requisite offices can be provided there without material expense.'

Steventon was chosen as being half way between London and Bristol; until the opening of the branch to Oxford it was regarded as an important first-class station. It did not remain the centre of Great Western government for long. The first meeting was held there on 21 July 1842 and the last on 5 January 1843. The directors had decided to concentrate all the company's business at London.

Brunel was asked to modify the superintendent's house for this purpose and when the management committees left, the building was used as general offices.

During this period, when trains terminated at Steventon, the service between Paddington and Steventon was at approximately two-hourly intervals – the first train leaving Paddington at 6am, reaching Steventon at 7.55 with the last train out at 8.57pm, also taking less than two hours for the journey. For travellers to Oxford the ensuing journey by road took one and a half hours for the ten miles.

Although the accomplishments so far had given great satisfaction there still remained the wrangling over the proposals for the Oxford line. This alone was the cause of the delay in laying the junction and building the new station, which was to be called Didcot Junction, thus settling the spelling of the name for ever.

The first opposition to the Oxford Railway came as far back as 1833 when the GWR first published its plans for the Bristol to London route. The opinion in Oxford was of faint surprise that a railway should even be proposed, but the reaction of the University was certainly predictable. The prospectus clause which was so disliked was that showing the actual line of the railway:

...which will pass through or near Slough, Reading, Wantage, Swindon... a branch only twelve miles long over level country may connect the main line to Oxford.

In 1841 the Revd J. Hodgkinson of Didcot wrote to the Principal of Brasenose College:

I wish we could come to a conclusion with this abominable set of men 'The Railway Company', for the perplexity they create is very disturbing indeed.

The arguments which ensued over the sale of the land both for the main line and the Oxford branch had caused him great concern. The Church was showing the strongest opposition to the sale of the land.

Brunel's determination to build a line to Oxford was far

more intense than at first it seemed. In a letter to the Board of Directors on 18 June 1839 he wrote:

The establishment of a central engine house at Reading not recommended, but if some point more concentral with reference to the whole distance between London and Bristol, such as Dudcot be considered more convenient. . .

To have been more central, as was his suggestion, was possibly another of his moves to get the Oxford junction in the locality of his choice. His ambition was to see a Great Western route through to Manchester, Liverpool and Birkenhead, thus covering the western side of the country. So, with the new junction in mind, did he have thoughts of developing Didcot with its engine house situated in a position to supply locomotives for both the main line and the north?

The directors' report to the half-yearly meeting in August 1836 stated:

A branch to Oxford and a continuation of it to Worcester are promoted by the leading interests of those two cities, and the best exertions of the Company will be devoted in co-operation with them to accomplish those objects.

This was again in the interests of Brunel in his quest to the north.

Although the bill for the Oxford line was promoted in the session of 1837 there was no further mention of a continuation to Worcester in the bill. As originally laid out the line started from Didcot and approached Cowley Road, Oxford, at a terminus near Magdalen Bridge and threw off a short branch to Abingdon. The proposal was strongly opposed by Christchurch College as owners of the land. To avoid this confrontation Brunel altered this terminus to a site near Folly Bridge. This, together with clauses in their favour, placated the College. The bill had an easy passage through the Commons, but in the Lords it met with such severe opposition from the owners of the land along the route that again it failed.

In 1838 the bill was revived and presented without the Abingdon branch. This had been abandoned as a result of the strenuous efforts of Mr Duffield, the MP for that borough, defending the landowners. The bill again passed the Commons but once more failed in the Lords, mainly by the intervention of the Duke of Wellington. In his speech to the Lords, his main reason for objecting to the railway to Oxford and possibly through to Worcester was '...because the railways encourage the lower classes to move about.'

After a further attempt in 1840 Oxford was still without the chance of a railway and the only means of travel was by stage coach.

Abingdon continued the pressure against the railway and refused to allow it to come anywhere near to the town. In the local newspaper of 18 February 1843 an article read:

At a meeting of the Town Council a resolution to dissent from the proposed Oxford and GWR was unanimously adopted. The line of the railway has given great disappointment to the town people and it is proposed to call a public meeting.

One month later another article highlighted opposition to the Oxford/Didcot Railway bill:

The public meeting held at the Guild Hall, proposal of presenting petition against the proposed branch of railway from Didcot to Oxford, the injurious effects on the town were pointed out. Unanimous vote against.

By the end of autumn of the same year a large proportion of the residents of Oxford, by contrast, had concluded that railways had been proven to be the best means of travel, the much quicker proposed service from Didcot being considered a great improvement. To this end the 1838 project was again revived.

During this period of wrangling, mainly because of the hostile attitude of the Abingdon people, George Stephenson had been commissioned by the London and Birmingham Railway to survey a route starting from Moulsford through Wallingford to Magdalen Bridge at Oxford, and this was being considered. As this particular terminus had been the stumbling block for the GWR the idea was rejected. By now the heads of the colleges voted on the matter. Only two of the twenty-three members sitting opposed the project – the strongest voice against belonging to the warden of Wadham College, this in his capacity as chairman of the Oxford Canal Company which stood to lose traffic to the railway. In general, the colleges were now more favourable to the railway project.

A bill was then deposited for the session of 1843 to incorporate the Oxford Railway Company and authorising the construction of the railway from the junction of Didcot to a certain field belonging to Brasenose College on the west of the Abingdon turnpike road. It seems ironic that after all the obstinate refusals by Brasenose College it should finally provide the terminus.

Several clauses were inserted into the bill at the insistence of the colleges, such as the preservation of university discipline, allowing chancellors, proctors, heads of colleges and their marshals to have free access at all times to the station to ascertain whether any of their members were travelling, or even attempting to, and forbade the company to allow anyone with a degree below that of master of arts or bachelor of civil law to travel.

The entire capital for the line was put up by the GWR thus eliminating shareholders, and power to sell or lease the line was also taken as early amalgamation was expected. The bill had an easy passage through Parliament and received the Royal Assent on 11 April 1843. Some difficulty was encountered obtaining some of the land in the area of Culham, which delayed the start of work until October of that year. The whole branch of nine miles fifty-seven chains was completed by June 1844, and on 10 June Major General Pasly, with Brunel and several directors, came down to inspect it. The line had been laid to the seven-foot gauge in common with the rest of the GWR, although at this time, what was commonly known as the gauge war was raging fiercely. Brunel fought hard for his broad gauge and with this new tentacle reaching out to the

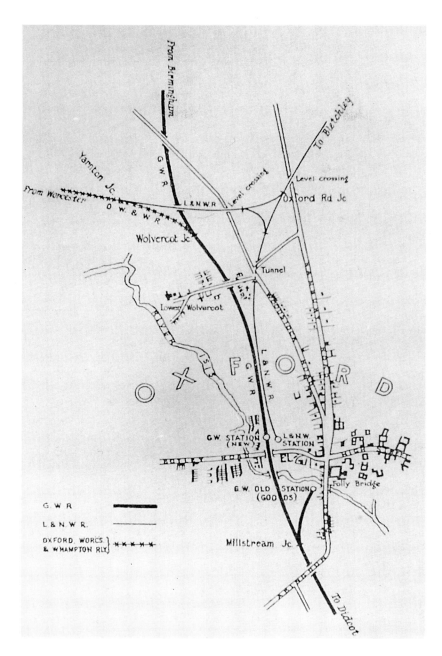

A map of Oxford in 1885 giving the line of the railway to its original 1844 terminus, shown here as *GW Old Station (Goods)*, and the additional lines to Worcester, Birmingham and the LNWR route into Oxford. *MacDermot's History*

north he could see the possibility of winning his point 'that the broad gauge made for safer running.'

It is worth remembering, that because of the GWR's original hope to run over L&BR standard-gauge metals into Euston, Brunel was well aware, from the beginning, of the arguments against two gauges in one relatively small country.

The *Oxford Times* printed on 15 June 1844:

Oxford and District Railway Company, this line being completed, Government inspector of railways General Pasly proceeded on Monday last by special train from Paddington to inspect the road and to report on its suitability. The distance from Paddington to Oxford is fifty-three miles and was performed in one hour eight minutes, accompanied by a large party, reaching Oxford about two o'clock. A large group of people waited at Folly bridge. Accordingly on Wednesday last, June 12, the line was opened. Thousands of people visited the line with great excitement. The country ride from Oxford to Didcot is very exceedingly beautiful but fares are much too high at 15s and 10s, more especially when the public can't sit. With charges of more than 5s the railway will be of no consequence to the working man.

On the same day of the opening of the Oxford line, 12 June 1844, the new station at Didcot Junction was also opened. Until then the local population had been deprived of rail travel – not that many in the area were in a position to use it at that time – but at least they could now look forward to some possible improvement and hope for prosperity.

The construction of the Oxford line had gone well, mainly due to the mild winter but the navvies caused their usual disturbances resulting in some of them being hauled in front of the magistrates. As the *Abingdon Herald* of 3 February 1844 recounted:

On Tuesday last a ruffian-looking fellow named Henry Parker but more generally known as 'Shiner' was up before S. Phillips Esq, a magistrate for Oxfordshire, charged with most violent and improper assault on Mr Josoph Ellis, an engineer employed on the railway now being built between Didcot and Oxford.

A later comment of 20 April 1844 referred to:

Three ruffianly fellows, Hayes, Williams, and Rogers, railway workers out of employment, charged with assault on a fellow worker who had been at work on the Appleford cutting of the railway, now in progress between Oxford and Didcot.

These cases mentioned were by no means isolated incidents. Wherever there were railway navvies there was certain to be trouble, their lives consisted of work for most of the day and when off there was nowhere to go but to the nearest inn. Brunel listed the evils affecting navvies as: the truck system – when a contractor paid his men in food and drink rather than money; irregular payment of the men; and excessive sub-letting of contracts. By comparison with local men they were in a position to consume much more ale, as a result they inevitably got drunk and fought, mainly amongst themselves.

The navvies at this time had no redress if, during their employment, they were injured; nor could their families demand compensation if they were killed.

In 1844 Parliamentary legislation decreed that third-class passengers should travel at no more than a penny a mile. Hence the name Parliamentary trains which were run to conform to this edict, the mode of travel being open wagons and more often than not without seats for the lower classes, in effect treated as cattle. The attitude shown to them was that if they could ride outside on a stage coach then they would be no worse off in an open truck.

As regards the possibility of falling out, the same applied – it was no different to falling off a stage coach. They were not alone with their hardships. The driver was also treated with some disdain, he and his fireman were thought of in the same manner as the stage-coach driver who also sat in the open. The driver and his mate had only a small footplate to ride on with, at the best, a handrail along each side and no cover in front to protect them from the elements driving into their faces at speed. The only respite from the winds and rain was to crouch down behind the firebox and to venture their heads out as necessary to look for signals. In these early days signals varied from place to place, some areas may have had the early disc-and-crossbar type while at other places a policeman with a flag was all that could be expected. Once again the attitude was adopted that the stage-coach drivers were out in the elements, notwithstanding the fact that trains were running much faster. There was also a brakesman riding on the back of the tender, but he was infinitely better off; he sat with his back to the engine to be in a position to observe the train and invariably had the protection of a high-backed seat.

These particular conditions were very slow to change; the men of those days were a very hardy breed.

EXETER EXPRESSES, 1845-1852

Miles from Paddington			10 Mar.–10 May 1845	12 May 1845–24 Jan 1846	26 Jan. 1846–Nov. 1847	Dec. 1847–Sept. 1848	Oct. 1848–April 1849	May 1849–Mar. 1852	April–Dec. 1852
	Down Train								
	Paddington	dep.	9 30	9 45	9 45	9 50	9 50	9 50	9 45
$52\frac{7}{8}$	Didcot	arr.	10 43	10 53	10 50	10 45	10 45	10 45	10 43
		dep.	10 45	10 55	10 52	10 47	10 47	10 47	10 45
77	Swindon	arr.	11 20	11 27	11 23	11 15	11 15	11 15	11 15
		dep.	11 30	11 28	11 33	11 25	11 25	11 25	11 25
$93\frac{3}{4}$	Chippenham		—	—	—	—	11 45	11 45	11 45
$106\frac{5}{8}$	Bath	arr.	12 10	12 6	12 9	12 0	12 5	12 5	12 10
		dep.	12 12	12 8	12 11	12 2	12 7	12 7	12 12
$118\frac{1}{4}$	Bristol	arr.	12 30	12 25	12 28	12 20	12 25	12 25	12 30
	(Express Platform)	dep.	12 35	12 30	12 33	12 25	12 30	B. & E. R. 12 30	12 35
$151\frac{5}{8}$	Bridgwater		—	—	—	1 5	1 9	*1 15	*1 15
163	Taunton	arr.	1 35	1 26	1 27	1 27	1 31		
		dep.	1 37	1 28	1 29	1 29	1 33	1 40	1 40
$193\frac{3}{4}$	Exeter	arr.	2 30	2 15	2 15	2 15	2 20	*2 30	*2 30
Miles. Intermediate	*Up Train*								
	Exeter	dep.	11 45	12 0	12 0	12 0	12 30	12 40	
$30\frac{3}{4}$	Taunton	arr.	12 30	12 41	12 41	12 40	1 9	*1 27	
		dep.	12 32	12 43	12 43	12 42	1 11	1 29	
$11\frac{1}{2}$	Bridgwater		—	—	—	12 58	1 27	1 45	
$33\frac{1}{4}$	Bristol	arr.	1 35	1 40	1 36	1 40	2 10	*2 35	
	(Express Platform)	dep.	1 40	1 45	1 41	1 44	2 14	G. W. R. 2 39	
$11\frac{5}{8}$	Bath	arr.	1 55	2 2	1 56	2 0	2 30	2 55	
		dep.	1 57	2 4	1 58	2 2	2 32	2 57	
13	Chippenham		—	—	—	—	2 52	3 17	
$16\frac{5}{8}$	Swindon	arr.	2 45	2 46	2 43	2 45	3 20	3 45	
		dep.	2 55	2 47	2 53	2 55	3 30	3 55	
$24\frac{1}{8}$	Didcot	arr.	3 28	3 18	3 22	3 22	3 57	4 22	
		dep.	3 30	3 20	3 24	3 25	4 0	4 25	
$52\frac{7}{8}$	Paddington	arr.	4 45	4 30	4 30	4 30	5 0	5 25	

It is uncertain whether the Chippenham and Bridgwater times are arrival or departure.

* Stops at Weston Junction and Tiverton Junction.

A timetable showing the down and up Exeter express between March 1845 and December 1852, which called at Didcot.

Steventon was hardest hit by the opening of the Oxford line, its fortunes changed when trains were able to run direct from London to Oxford. Passengers from the West of England were also able to change at Didcot, indeed all the passengers for Oxford were now able to complete their journey by train. It is recorded that in 1842, for example, this station dealt with 77,567 passengers and 12,630 tons of goods traffic. All this passenger and goods traffic fell off with the opening of Didcot, leaving Steventon to fall into decline as a small village station.

The station eventually closed to passenger traffic on 7 December 1964. Goods services continued until 29 March 1965.

There is little now to indicate that a station, once so important, existed, except that the original Brunel built London offices and the station master's house still survive as listed buildings.

The station's status as a terminus lasted less than six weeks. On 20 July 1840 the line was opened to Faringdon Road (later Challow). This was another indication of Brunel's resolve to get a junction to the north, his haste to provide a station at Steventon as a staging point for Oxford. This determination was strong enough to make Steventon a terminal requiring locomotive facilities, such as water supply and a turntable, with his certain knowledge that it would be operational for a short period only, until the line was carried through. This is borne out by his previous comment:

Beyond Dudcot great exertions have been made to complete the line for an opening to a point near Farington simultaneously with the opening to Reading, the opening may be calculated June or early July.

At his time of writing the turntable was also being constructed, knowing it to be required for such a short period.

It has never been exactly clear just where the turntable was situated but a quote from the *GWR Magazine* gives a good indication:

In those days the locomotives were turned in a space in front of the existing station. A portion of the original track (reduced in gauge, of course) is actually still in use at the station.

This line is most likely to be the unloading dock adjacent to the up platform at the west end.

Speculation also exists regarding the water supply. Water would certainly have been taken from the nearby Ginge Brook, or river as it was sometimes called. I have in my mind some distant memory of seeing a small flat-topped mushroom water tank to the rear of the yard. This possibility is confirmed by Mr Ken Ellis who is the son of a more recent station master of Steventon and lived in the station house with his parents from a very young age. He recalls seeing a large concrete square at the rear of the stables with water pipes coming from it, which

may have served as a base for the tank column.

To the west end of the sidings a goods shed was placed, but it seems that it was not there for some considerable time after the station was built, it had a standard gauge opening for a through line to the rear. This shed was supplied with wagons from the Didcot 'fly' goods each day. Many times have I been into this little shed as a fireman depositing vehicles.

To the rear of the shed there was a considerable stable block for the benefit of the company's horses – the stage coach operators supplying their own.

Langfords the coal merchants also had offices and a weigh-bridge set on the back road and further along Bookers had a corn and feed store in a rather impressive barn, as it was referred to. For some reason it was also called Bradfields Mill and was served by a small wagon turntable with a short spur to the building. The turntable sat in a very precarious position very near to the edge of the brook, and the building, although in use, was very dilapidated in my time, during the war years.

From the opening in 1840 the station was in the hands of Mr Beck who held the position of station master until his retirement in 1876 when he was succeeded by his son Mr G.A. Beck, after only three years in the company's service at Steventon; he in turn retired in 1920. Mr Belcher followed and Mr Pearce completed the chain.

One feature which stands out in my memory of Steventon was the divisional boundary post which was situated some hundred yards on the up side of the line to the east of the road bridge. It was in the form of a large gradient board with the words **Bristol Division** to the west and **London Division** to the east. Later the divisional boundary was moved to Challow.

The station was built by Messrs Rigby. The small station building was unusual in not having a canopy on the platform side yet having one on the road side for the benefit of the stage-coach passengers. On the down side the only accommodation was the usual GWR open 'pagoda' which was reached by crossing the road bridge. Later the pagoda was replaced by the type of shelter with a curved roof.

Oxford passengers and goods were still dealt with at Steventon until the opening of Didcot Junction in June 1844. Mails from the West of England continued to unload from the 7pm Penzance Travelling Post Office, calling at 2.15am. Then by the time-honoured road journey, the A34, to Oxford. This service was withdrawn towards the end of March 1962, trains then stopped at Didcot.

Soon after this the station was demolished together with the signal box, goods shed and other buildings. All was swept away, leaving only the original general offices and the station master's house of what was once an important, albeit, short lived prelude to Didcot.

Platelayers at Steventon Crossing c1890.   *Author's collection*

Loco No.564 with crew and station staff pose for the camera during shunting operations in Steventon yard c1910. The loco was built at Wolverhampton in 1896, withdrawn 1933. Fitted with R4S type boiler in 1931, some of this type were also fitted for auto-working. The loco was allocated at Didcot at this time but ended its days at Leamington.
                                                                              Ken Ellis

Above: Impressive Churchward 2-8-0 No.4705 stands at Steventon on 13 May 1961, while the crew pose for their picture. The loco, based at Plymouth Laira, appears to be in ex-works condition and is working a Didcot to Swindon stopping passenger, a favourite turn for newly-shopped engines.

Further along the line, No.4705 stands at Challow on the same train.

Both R C Riley

CHAPTER FIVE

The Junction Station

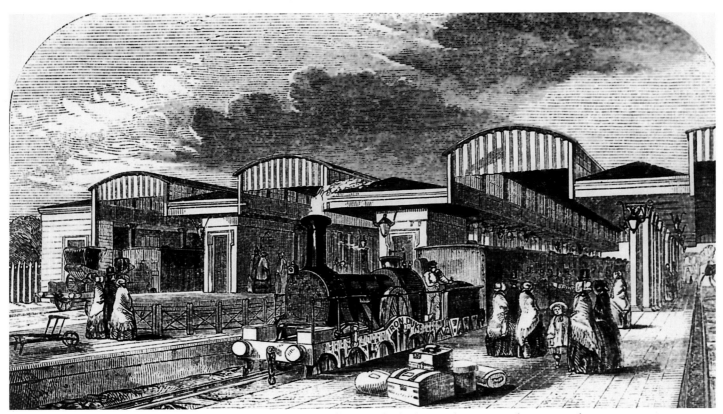

The only illustration available of the original Brunel station showing the high ventilators over the running lines.

Mason's Guide to GWR Sept. 1885

With the opening of the Oxford line in June 1844 this rather grand station was also opened – although it was not always given this accolade – so that Brunel must have seen his ambitions coming to fruition, his dreams of a line to the north being complemented by such a large edifice. It rated second only to the Paddington and Temple Meads stations at the ends of the line – quite a large station, more than comparable to Reading, because of its important junction.

The station, in common with all the others on the line was constructed of wood in the main, but, unlike Reading, all the platforms were together under one roof span. The station stood on a higher level than the road alongside. Indeed there was no road at that time, only a cart track cum footpath.

The earthworks to maintain the level of the railway track were excavated from the cutting at Moreton and a little from the cutaway embankment alongside the line west of the station as far as Foxhall bridge and a short way beyond.

In the early 1850s a clerk came to work at Didcot, after which he wrote in his memoirs about the station and its vicinity. He had been employed by the railway in varying capacities in and around Didcot for a number of years. Not wishing to be identified, he wrote under the pseudonym of Ernest Struggles. It was some years later that some of his contemporaries who knew of him, were able to give credence to his story. He described several of the locations at which he had worked, giving each of them fictitious names but still his web of intrigue was penetrated, and there seems no doubt that what he attributes to Didcot is genuine, not fiction. For this reason I would like to include extracts from his very vivid account of what the station and its work was really like in the early years.

He recalls the day when he first arrived at Didcot to take up his new appointment. After alighting from the train he looked for someone in authority to ask directions to the station master's office. In his anxiety to please he went to the nearest person who appeared to have authority, a gentleman wearing a tall hat and long coat tails. Unfortunately Ernest Struggles failed to give the respect due to such a high-standing person and was quite set back when the same person identified himself as the one for whom he was asking. Ernest relates how he got off to a very poor start with his new boss, taking some considerable time to gain his respect and recognition.

He wrote of the station master:

He had an extraordinary gait and appearance. Although very tall, he lost quite two inches by stooping. But for an occasional shout such as, 'Are you all right that side; now then, get in: What are you at?' I should not only fail to recognise my superior officer, but I would probably have taken him for a tramp. He had aquiline hard features and straight hair. With his tall hat and coat tails he presented an unusual figure as a station master.

The station master's call to the staff, 'Are you all right that side', was because passengers could board or alight either side on some platforms.

Describing the station he continued:

It was a junction and passengers changed here, for everywhere on the Great Western Railway. The trains from the west came here to meet trains from the north, and vice versa.

These writings were relating to the time when the station had settled down to some sort of routine, fifteen or so years after opening. They show that by the 1860s the station was in full swing with a considerable amount of activity, as this extract shows:

Stopping trains and expresses were dealt with and connecting services were of great importance. Stopping trains were shunted for express trains to pass, the cheap up and down trains shunted and held for an hour and a half, as it was the practice in those days to run one cheap or third class only in each direction.

It is believed that the reason for such delaying tactics was to force people to pay second or first class fares:

What with stopping, changing trains and starting, Didcot junction was a very busy place. The station itself was like a dirty old barn, with the ends knocked out to allow trains to run through; the roofing was blackened with smoke, and the paint was blistering. There were four roads for trains to stand under this roof, or, strictly speaking, in the station, and five very narrow platforms.

The only communication between the platforms was by an eight foot wide subway, which itself was very filthy from engines above leaking oil and water. Some directions were painted on the walls which were unreadable, causing no end of problems to passengers.

As Ernest Struggles was a clerk he was concerned about others and the positions they held. In his observations he wrote:

There was a goods shed and an engine shed, but the work of the goods office was transacted in a room adjoining the booking office, not that it should be a source of comfort for the clerks, but in order that the two duties might be combined, to save expense.

The entrance to the station seems to have been as it was until the recent refurbishment, entering by the subway to the booking office just inside:

The station master had a private office upstairs on the platform. Because of Didcot's importance as a junction the number of tickets issued was ten times more than that of an ordinary wayside station. The booking office was of a different nature, the most unfortunate part was that the counter was an open one without any shelter for the clerk, not the usual pigeon hole. In frosty weather the ink froze in the well... It was the custom to take the day's receipts to the goods clerk at night. He received £70 per annum, and was therefore designated the senior officer; the booking clerk received £60 per annum.

By this time the *Junction Hotel* had been built opposite the station together with some other inns. Didcot was only a little village, and the engine drivers, porters, and the guards had already monopolised every house in the place therefore lodgings were difficult to find; one room, solely for sleeping, cost Ernest 3s6d a week.

In a further appraisal of the station master, Ernest wrote:

Invariably the station master did not arrive on the platform until about ten-thirty, at which time the down express came in, afterwards read his letters, then distributed them, after which he went to the hotel opposite for his luncheon. At one o'clock the up express came in after which he went to dinner until four o'clock. The trains were usually thick at this time and at six o'clock he went to tea and went to his office and sat until midnight.

The night foreman was regarded as the night station master for which he received an extra £1 a week. Unfortunately, for reading well and writing was not a requirement for the job, therefore promotion prospects were unlikely.

Of the station master's duties Ernest soon found out which was the most objectionable to him; that was the enquiries which he had to make repeatedly of the locomotive superintendent, reporting the engine drivers for petty negligences, which brought him into contempt with the establishment. As a result the booking clerk was given the task of visiting the shed at all hours to get the necessary information.

Ernest, it seems, had an affinity with the locomen when he wrote of his feelings for them:

Of all the men in the railway company's employ there is no class of which we are so little acquainted, and yet in the coaching days the driver was the man whose society

No.2361 double framed Dean 0-6-0 outside the old shed, October 1931, with the sand furnace on the right. *V R Webster*

was most sought. Is it not again astonishing, whereas the driver of a coach and four horses, value a few hundred pounds, and say twenty passengers, should come from the middle classes, that the driver of a railway engine and train, with say one hundred passengers and so many thousand pounds worth of property, should come from from the lower order?

It was astonishing for him to see the material from which the engine drivers sprang:

On the Great Western Railway they began as a lad seeking work as a night engine cleaner; if he got on well it was a great promotion to him to be a lighter-up. The next step was to that as a fireman to a goods driver, and if there was nothing to prevent it, he got to be appointed to a shunting engine in time, then on to a stopping passenger train and lastly, you might easily pin on the word 'lastly', to an express train. It is simply marvellous that with such training we have at this present day such an immense number of worthy men as engine drivers. Very few better class men in 1860 would have undergone such an ordeal to reach this position. While an educated man writes as a clerk at 20s a week, an engine driver rides by him, with no social pretentions, at double the money, and enjoys his occupation. They are marvels of manufacture, they know nothing of steam but they know a great deal about the working parts of an engine, they will pack an old crock to keep it going with loving care, whereas a scientific, educated man would not even risk his life for such an old blunderbuss.

One point not mentioned by Ernest Struggles was that locomen of that time, particularly goods trainmen, had no reasonable roster of turns and as such found themselves being sent for to work as and when they were required – in short, arriving home again at the whim of the foreman. There was no consideration for the employee and his home life, only the good of the company. A recognised rest period was unheard of, men were expected to return to work as and when they were asked.

The shed he knew and wrote about stood some hundred yards on the northern side of the station and was reached from the far exit of the subway and then by a footpath which ran alongside the shunting yard. It was built originally with two roads, each long enough to accommodate several small tender engines, those in for maintenance. Other locomotives were stabled outside while waiting duty. A shed had been built at the same time as the station to supply engines for the Oxford branch, bearing in mind Brunel's letter suggesting that an engine house at Didcot would be more concentrical. This small shed survived until the 1850s when it was replaced by a much more substantial structure, but again having only two roads; in later years an additional road was added on the northern side in the form of a lean-to with the pitch of the original roof continuing down at the same angle over the new section to its outside wall.

Many of the drivers with whom I worked during my early days at Didcot talked of this shed, mainly in respect of the poor conditions; lack of ventilation and very shallow inspection pits were the worst problems. The poor pits gave the more portly drivers some difficulty when crawling underneath to oil the motion.

The railway company with some considerable foresight built its own gas producing plant, locating it within the boundary of the loco shed, situated at the rear of the coal stage. The works supplied gas for the engine shed, the lighting within the sidings, and also for the station and the shunting yard. Those passenger coaches which were lit by gas were also charged from this plant. There was a coal stage with a stop block at the end of the road. This was a simple building consisting only of a small platform where coal was shovelled on from wagons on one side and then shovelled on to the tenders on the other side as required. A metal framed structure covered the roof with the roof extending a little way over the tender as a canopy.

The turntable was situated on the road leading into the engine shed, incoming engines had to pass over it to enter the shed. In addition all coaching stock was obliged to pass over the table towards the carriage shed except for the two roads on the northern side. In this position both engines and coaches could use the same turntable.

In addition to this there was a water tank near the table which stood high on two very strong walls with a siding passing through below, towards the rear of the shed.

The passenger shed was extensive with seven quite long roads, the company going to great lengths to keep the coaching stock under cover, whereas the engines were stabled mainly outside. The layout of the engine and carriage shed remained basically the same until the whole area was rebuilt in 1932.

The first known foreman of the new shed built in the early 1850s was named Jim Hill, who became a legend to many men. His duties covered the responsibilities of the shed in much the same way as the station master did at the station, and he was in attendance for most of the day. Jim Hill was followed by a series of men whose christian names were never mentioned, Mr Swallow first then Mr Davies, Mr Samsworth, Mr Dowding, Mr Wyatt, Mr Saunders and then Bill Young, he being the man who arrived at Didcot the same day as myself in October 1939. The difference was that he was taking up the most senior position while I filled the position of the most junior fireman. As years passed by, shift foremen were appointed to run the shed during the afternoon and night, while the chief took care of the daytime working.

At this time there was a small goods shed to the side of the down main line, a little to the west of the station, which was reached by a siding from the main line and also from the road outside, to receive and dispatch parcels and goods. Delivery outside the station must have been of a very limited nature as the roads in the area were little better than cart tracks. This is the shed which was referred to by Ernest Struggles with its office at the station next to the booking office.

The station horse for drawing the delivery cart was stabled on the opposite side of the station front near to the slip road leading up to the east end loading dock. Adjoining the goods shed on a slightly lower level there was a small coal yard, which, particularly in those days, would have served only those most affluent in the area. Later, with the better-paid railwaymen now moving in, several small coal merchants started business – the first signs of prosperity in the area.

The main trade in the area was of sheep and some cattle, the coming of the railway breathed new life into their business, the local farmers now had the facility to take their trade further afield, using the loading dock for this purpose.

A flock of sheep being driven past the Corn Exchange, now the YMCA, towards the cattle pens dock at the east end bay.

Author's collection

49

The *Great Western Junction Hotel* opposite the station.

Author's collection

The railway certainly brought in more trade and in 1857 a cornmarket was built to the west side of the station, near to the small yard. The sheep market grew and more buyers were coming to the market for the local auctions. There was still no accommodation to be had in the village but this situation was soon remedied by the building of the *Junction Hotel* opposite the station. Better facilities were needed; there were none in the old village and very little on the turnpike road. When the construction workers had moved on the new railway employees moved in and were reasonably happy to suffer the frugal conditions to be able to secure such lucrative work. Many of the drivers were drafted initially from areas of heavy machinery manufacture – men who would be better equipped to understand the workings of a steam engine.

Work on the farms now took second place, there was a keenness on the part of the local youth to seek employment with the railway. This in turn put a strain on the farmers, who were hard pushed to get young lads to take on the long hours for so little pay, at the same time the situation served to eliminate those not suitable for the railway.

Changes did not come quickly, it was some time before they saw any improvement. About 1890 the village was blessed with some new houses built by a local man solely for the purpose of letting; they were in the form of a short row of terrace cottages built at the eastern end of the village and served their purpose for well over a hundred years.

The station had been built solely for the purpose of passengers changing trains from east/west to the north and vice versa. The possibility of any large number of travellers joining at Didcot was very remote.

The railway company realised that with the turnpike road passing just a little way away there was a reasonable hope that some business might be generated by having a road to connect it to the station. To this end Brunel built a road in 1846 and named it Station Hill. Soon after this another local builder built a large row of terrace houses on the turnpike road – which was now called Wallingford Road – at the junction of Station Hill. This enterprise was named Mount Pleasant, at the time an apt name with only the local cottages to compare with. The main occupants of this terrace were railwaymen, and with this concentration of men in one employ the buildings soon became known as the 'Barracks' but for some reason did not survive for any great length of time.

Following closely in 1847 the *White Hart Inn* was built on the opposite corner to Mount Pleasant, and as time passed more hotels were provided opposite the station and also a public house, more in keeping with the needs of the workers.

North Hagbourne. Wallingford Road looking down.

Author's collection

In a letter as early as 1846, T.H. Bertram, chief assistant to Brunel, wrote to Seymore Clarke, enclosing sketches from Brunel, of suggested cottages to be built in Station Hill. In the event forty odd years elapsed before these houses were eventually built, but it does show the concern which the railway had for its employees.

There was another road into Didcot which came in from the Oxford direction via Abingdon and Appleford and curving round from the east through a lane known as Lydalls Lane and on in a westerly direction into the village; the new Station Hill bisected this lane at a point just east of the station.

More houses were built at an area known as Hagbourne Marsh on the Wallingford road, near to where the railway crossed. Again these were built as speculation, by George Napper, who charged rather high rents; as a consequence, in common with other highly priced accommodation, it effectively reserved them for the better-off railwaymen. Old Didcot, as it was now becoming known, was becoming more and more isolated, creating two separate communities, the railwaymen to the east and the local farm workers to the west.

Tucked in behind the corn exchange the little goods shed handled all the local goods traffic and possibly some for the market, but across the line to the north and a little way to the west of the station, just beyond the Oxford line junction there stood another goods shed. This shed had no connection with the outside movement of goods, it was concerned solely with the transfer of goods from one wagon to another.

A situation had arisen because of the rivalry between the various railway companies as to which was the most suitable gauge to adopt as standard. As we know, Brunel stood alone in his insistence that his broad 7ft gauge was far safer than the generally accepted standard gauge and refused to surrender his opinion. Having laid all his main line with the broad gauge, followed by the line to Oxford, he was spurred on with his ambition to continue to the north and saw that if this came about his strength of argument lay in the fact that the Great Western would be the largest individual company and would sway the argument in his favour – notwithstanding the fact that the rest of the railway companies in concert would have the overall majority.

While these quarrels were fomenting, the situation at Didcot remained very difficult. All the time that lines in and out of Didcot had remained compatible there was no problem, but when, in December 1856, a number of routes were either laid as mixed gauge or converted to such, difficulties arose. There was now the possibility of direct transit from south to north on what had become the standard gauge of 4ft 8½in, starting at Basingstoke on the LSWR via Reading and, above all, the Great Western main line to Didcot and Oxford.

The Gauge Act, 1846, forebade any railway company to construct a railway for the conveyance of passengers on any gauge other than 4ft 8½in. Brunel, however, with his eyes to the north, and already having certain arrangements with the Oxford, Worcester & Wolverhampton Railway for a broad gauge, never gave up his quest.

The gauge war, or battle of the gauges, as it became known, came to a head in 1844 with the meeting of the gauges at Gloucester, between the Great Western and the Birmingham & Gloucester Railway. Also in 1844 the GWR decided to take a broad gauge line direct from Oxford to Worcester and on to Wolverhampton. Accordingly on 20 September they made an agreement between themselves and the Oxford, Worcester & Wolverhampton Railway.

The London & Birmingham Railway also promoted a line to Worcester and Wolverhampton, to run via Bicester, Fenny Compton, and Evesham with branches to Oxford. They also proposed a branch from Oxford to Didcot to join with the South Western line at Basingstoke. With the abandonment of the latter, the bill was withdrawn.

All these threats of incursions into the territory which Brunel had hoped to dominate spurred him on. He doggedly followed his opinion that the broad gauge was far superior and safer.

The gauge war showed no signs of abating, both camps attacking and counter attacking until in 1845 a Royal Commission on the Gauge of Railways was formed. They opened their proceedings on 6 August 1845. Brunel faced the commission with a great deal of confidence and not a little bravado; his spirited counter attacks however failed to convince the commissioners. In turn Gooch stood alone against the combined strength of the narrow gauge protagonists, defending the power and capabilities of his broad gauge engines. Eminent men such as Robert Stephenson, Joseph Locke, G.P. Bidder and others were ranged against him.

After nearly three months of fierce arguments Brunel threw out a challenge, 'That the merits of the respective engines be put to a practical test', to which the commission agreed. This apparently sporting offer was firmly backed by both Brunel and Gooch's belief that their engines were superior.

For the tests the narrow gauge representatives proposed a line from York to Darlington, 44 miles, and from Paddington to Didcot for the GWR a distance of 53 miles. Gooch pressed for a more exacting route, suggesting Paddington to Bristol, a normal service route, but the narrow gauge companies declined and the commissioners agreed.

The GWR, who had not received any new engines since 1842 relied on one of their regular service engines. Gooch chose Ixion, one of his 7ft singles as his champion, built by Fenton, Murray & Jackson of Leeds in 1841 with cylinders of 15¾ inches by 18 inches stroke, and a boiler pressure of 75lbs per square inch, an amount agreed to for the tests.

Gooch's Ixion ran three double trips between Paddington and Didcot on 16/17 December. On the first down journey with a load of eight coaches of ten tons each, the maximum speed attained was 53mph, the second trips with 70 tons, gave similar figures. The third journey, with 60 tons, was performed from start to stop in 63 minutes 34 seconds, at an average speed of 50mph, with a maximum of 60mph. The up journey to the fifty mile-post took 57 minutes 55 seconds, average speed 53.9, maximum 61mph.

Brunel treated the tests as a competition to show which gauge was most suitable. In reality it was the power and performance of the engines which was the real issue; the opposition realised this and had new locomotives ready in an effort to prove their point. The narrow gauge engine was known as Engine A, a Stephenson 'long boiler' No 54, recently built with 6ft 6in wheels and cylinders 15 inch by 21 inch stroke. This engine took a load of 40 tons from York to Darlington and back in the morning of 31 December and 80 tons to Darlington only in the afternoon. The trial of No 54 on the following day terminated in a derailment after only twenty five miles, although it had previously reached a speed of 60mph with 40 tons. The rest of the trials were also a failure for the narrow gauge; the maximum speed attained on any trip was 54mph with 50 tons.

The commissioner's report, laid before Parliament in the session of 1846, was, in part, a vindication of Gooch, although, once again, the forthrightness of Brunel earned him much of the credit:

We consider the trials as confirming the statements and results given by Mr Gooch, in his evidence, proving, as they do, that the broad gauge engines possess greater capabilities for speed with equal loads, and generally speaking, of propelling greater loads with equal speeds; and moreover that the working of such engines is economical where very high speeds are required, or where the loads to be conveyed are such as to require the full power of the engine.

We feel it a duty to observe here that the public are mainly indebted for the present rate of speed to the genius of Mr Brunel, and the liberality of the Great Western Railway.

Nevertheless the broad gauge lost its case, as the commissioners were convinced by the narrow gauge lobby:

That it would be dangerous for the broad gauge to be allowed to run any faster, and that the standard gauge possessed the greater convenience, and was more suited to the traffic of the country.

The commissioners summed up their conclusions as to the need for uniformity of gauge by saying:

We consider a break in the gauge to be a very serious evil, that no method has been proposed which is calculated to remedy, in any important degree, the inconvenience of attending a break in the gauge, and the general adoption of such a system ought not to be adopted.

The commissioners, while admitting the superiority of the broad gauge, were generally in favour of the narrow and went so far as to recommend:

... that equitable means should be found of establishing uniformity by the compulsory extinction of the broad gauge.

The commission made their final decision saying:

There could not be two main line gauges in the country, for the benefit of uninterrupted communications from north to south, and from east to west, one of them had to go.

They also appreciated the value of express trains but in the interests of uniformity they recommended:

...an alteration of the broad gauge to narrow gauge, more especially when we take into consideration that the broad gauge is only 274 miles long compared with 1901 of narrow.

Even at this stage they asked Brunel for his opinion on the subject, to which he replied '...that a single additional rail should be laid.' In effect he was now recommending a mixed gauge, almost as if he was capitulating, but he fought on. It seems odd that Brunel himself should make this suggestion which would eventually sound the death knell of the broad gauge.

On 4 July 1845 the committee decided 'that the preambles of the Oxford, Worcester & Wolverhampton Railway bill be approved'. This was, of course, a great victory for the broad gauge, but it was tempered with a clause obliging the GWR to add a narrow gauge line throughout.

Gooch wrote on the conflict:

This year began our hardest gauge fight. The Great Western went to Parliament for a line from Oxford to Worcester and Wolverhampton. This was to be broad gauge but was strongly opposed by the Birmingham Company. I had to give evidence on the bill and prepared very elaborate tables showing the speed and economy of the gauge... three weeks later they gave us the bill 4 July.

I will never forget the passion George Stephenson got into when the decision of the committee was announced he gave me his mind very freely for fighting the broad gauge against the narrow, on which he said, 'I had been reared'.

Brunel caused a clause to be inserted in the Gauge Act which became law on 18 August, establishing the standard gauge at 4ft 8 1/2 inches, but at the same time he was able to continue laying the broad gauge of 7ft, such as on the OW&W where these conditions were laid down. Having fought for so long and so hard it soon became a hollow victory.

Gooch's final comment was:

This was the last of the real fights... but as the proportion of broad gauge to narrow is so small, there is no doubt the country must submit to a gradual displacement of the broad gauge, and the day will come when it will cease.

To keep traffic on the Great Western from the west to the north it became necessary to transfer goods from broad gauge to standard gauge wagons, and vice versa. To do this with the least disturbance and to keep the goods dry a suitable shelter was needed. Brunel built a shed in 1863 – the transfer shed – which was quite extensive, each of the two roads holding about six wagons. The road nearest to the main line was laid to accommodate broad-gauge vehicles and ran right through the open end to the goods yard at the rear. The other line on the northern side was the narrower standard gauge, shown by the fact that it was not wide enough to admit a broad gauge vehicle; possibly the first

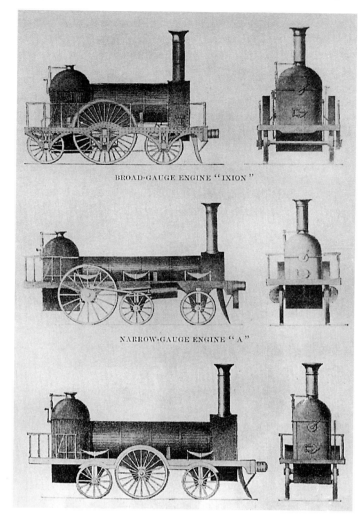

BROAD-GAUGE ENGINE "IXION"

NARROW-GAUGE ENGINE "A"

Gooch's broad gauge engine *Ixion* which took part in the gauge trials on 16/17 December 1845 between Paddington and Didcot. The engines known as 'A' and No.54 were competitors from other railway companies. *MacDermot's History*

piece of standard gauge only (as opposed to mixed gauge) line laid at Didcot, and by Brunel himself. This line ended at the stop blocks inside the far end of the shed. Outside, behind the wall, the offices stood with a door up to the central platform.

The platform was approximately 12ft wide, goods to be transferred were manhandled across the platform mainly on two-wheeled sack trucks. Goods which were too heavy were transported across by one of three cranes situated along the platform. These cranes, as I remember them, were quite unusual; they stood in the centre of the platform, their stout wooden columns rising to about 12ft. The jib was formed with two curved steel strips attached at the base and supported by straight steel bars at the top. A reduction gear was effected by a small drum at waist height with turning handles and connected to a large pulley at the top which drove another small drum with the hoisting chain turning on it. The effect enabled a man to lift the maximum load of one ton with little effort.

When eventually the standard gauge was established and the shed was no longer needed, it was put to more useful work as a goods depot, replacing the small shed across the other side of the main line. This was fortuitous, as goods traffic was gradually increasing and larger facilities were required. To the men, it always remained the transfer shed, right to the end.

I well remember, when it was in full use as a goods shed, walking through on many occasions between the wagons and the outside wall where there was ample room left by the removal of the broad gauge line.

When goods traffic was reduced to such a small amount in the early 1970s, the work of the shed was discontinued. In 1979 BR presented it to the Great Western Society who, with great care, had it dismantled and re-erected in their compound.

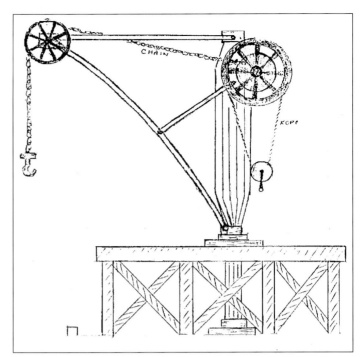

A sketch of the original cranes used in the transfer shed, as remembered by the author.

The transfer shed, disused, but still occupying its original position next to the running lines.   *W Pereira*

54

CHAPTER SIX

Changing Needs

The gradual introduction of mixed gauge track was accelerated in 1856 with the introduction of several new sections which were important to the changing needs of Didcot. These included the Didcot loop – now referred to as the avoiding line – which was laid as mixed gauge and opened 22 December, together with the Reading loop from Reading West junction to Oxford Road junction on the same date.

Also on the same date Oxford Road junction to Basingstoke, and Reading West junction to Oxford Isis Bridge were both converted to mixed gauge.

It was seven years later, on 1 June 1863, when the section from Didcot East junction through the station, and the continuation to the North junction, a total distance of only 1.12 miles, was opened for mixed traffic.

On 26 November 1872 two sections – Didcot station to Oxford (64m.p.), a distance of 10 miles 71 chains, and Didcot loop, East junction to North junction, 1 mile 2 chains, were again converted, this time to standard gauge. The 66 chain line from Oxford Millstream junction to the old station was closed on this day also.

The line from Didcot to Swindon, 24 miles 73 chains, was converted to mixed gauge in February 1872, thus completing the overall use of mixed gauge vehicles in the Didcot area. Mixed gauge track now radiated in each direction, east, west and north; now there was no need for the transfer shed.

The additional convenience of being able to move through traffic direct from west to north was accomplished when the junction was completed from Foxhall to the west curve on 15 February 1886. The mixed gauge situation continued until 1892, when on the weekend of 20/23 May all the main lines were converted to standard gauge; a total of 423 miles.

As far back as 1845 grandiose ideas had been floated regarding a railway line to connect the important port of Southampton with the industrial north. At that time, several routes had been suggested, all part of the railway mania of the day. The one which seemed the most likely to succeed was the proposed Oxford, Southampton, Gosport & Portsmouth Railway, leaving the LSWR at Micheldever, and following a route which passed near Aldermaston and across to Didcot, over country which had no towns to serve.

Doubts were raised regarding the viability of such a line, bearing in mind that the traffic which would use this route, was already being carried on the LSWR via Basingstoke and on to Reading, then on through Didcot to the north. Through lack of finance the plan failed, but was not buried.

Newbury, at that time, was a thriving market town, the centre of the local market industry, only a few miles from Aldermaston, so why should it have been by-passed?

The area mainly grew cereal crops, with a large proportion being barley, as the many malt houses in the district bore witness to. Horses, cattle, and pigs complemented the economy.

The prospect of a wider market gave incentive to the local traders to back a railway scheme. The railway directors themselves were more concerned with the lucrative business of carrying the industrial produce of the north to Southampton.

When the line from Oxford (Millstream junction) was completed to Banbury in 1850, interest was again aroused, and when five years later, the line to Worcester and Wolverhampton was finally opened throughout in the summer of 1855, much more urgency was generated. Even so, it was almost another twenty years before the Didcot & Southampton Railway was promoted, but due to lack of financial backing there was delay in getting the bill through Parliament. It eventually succeeded, and, on 26 August 1879, the work was commenced with the first sod being turned by Lady Carnarvon. The railway was at last under way with much rejoicing from the inhabitants of Newbury. The Didcot Newbury & Southampton Railway, as it was now called, followed a different route, veering away from Aldermaston, taking a more direct line to Winchester, later to be joined to the LSWR by a short branch from Shawford junction, and from there to run over that line to Southampton.

This route seems to have been somewhat ambitious, when bearing in mind that one reason for the initial failures had been the type of country the line would have to negotiate. The main object of the line was to create a trunk road for speedy transit. To achieve this the line would need to be as straight and as level as possible. This would involve making deep cuttings or negotiating heavy gradients, or alternatively making long detours, either of which would be very expensive and defeat the object.

Mixed gauge was a fact of life around Didcot and area for years until the massive conversion to standard gauge only in May 1892. East of Didcot on the GW main line is Pangbourne station seen above in 1892, with mixed gauge, just prior to conversion to four roads, looking west, with the original footbridge bearing the GWR motif; and below in 1893, now converted to four roads and standard gauge. This view looking east shows the relief lines and, just below the veranda, the new up main line signal can be seen. *Mrs Iris Moon*

At the same time there was a need to serve as many local communities as possible. In the event there were only two towns of any consequence on the section between Newbury and the junction with the LSWR at Shawford. This section had no less than eleven gradients of 1 in 106 throughout its length, and many of a lesser degree, all of which served to restrict the train loading, and therefore reduce the payload. Very little seemed to be in their favour, the one redeeming feature, as they saw it, was that the line was now six miles shorter.

John Fowler was the Engineer for the line and Messrs Falkiner & Tancred were the contractors. John Fowler was responsible for making some alterations to the Newbury end of the line, using the Great Western station by making a bay line without a junction to the main line.

Local interest was kept alive, when on 28 July 1881, the directors employed a special train to inspect the completed section as far as Compton, half way from Newbury. On this occasion the company had no locomotives of its own, so the train was hauled by a contractors engine, a Manning Wardle 0-6-0ST, No.662 of 1877, appropriately named *Newbury*.

The remainder of the line took another nine months to complete, and on 12 April 1882 the official opening took place with a grand farewell from the people of Newbury. Bands played and the town was bedecked with flowers and bunting. Newbury had waited a long time for this day and celebrated in style.

The train departed from Newbury carrying local dignitaries and directors, leaving at 12.10 midday calling at Hermitage, Hampstead Norris, Compton, Upton and on to Didcot, where it arrived at 1.5pm The eighteen miles took fifty-five minutes, including the four stops. All along the line people were out to see the passing of the first train, and each of the country stations was decorated with flags. Didcot went a little further, they not only had flags and buntings, but hung large banners with the words, 'Wishing prosperity to the railways.'

Prosperity for the new line, they hoped, would now give them chance to expand their business, and the GWR would also be able to take advantage of the junction at Didcot, which would give them what they had always been struggling for, their opportunity to monopolise the traffic to the north.

In the meantime the GWR had acquired the Shrewsbury & Chester Railway, together with running powers into Manchester. This latest acquisition gave rise to the line north from Didcot station being called the Chester line.

The original intention was to lay a double line, in the event, due to lack of finance, only a single line was laid, but between Didcot and Newbury provision was made for doubling at a later date by purchasing sufficient land and making cuttings and overbridges wide enough to accommodate a double track. In later years the GWR agreed to work the line for a participation in the revenue.

After all the lengthy arguments and complications of getting the line built, it appears that it was the respected

The Victorian station at Upton & Blewbury on the DN&S, 11 May 1957, with the canopy renewed and a new lamp hut. The top of the signal box can be seen above the up line shelter.

R M Casserley

2625. G.W.R. Station, Newbury.

Newbury station as original two roads in 1890, soon after the opening of the Lambourn branch with the signals to the left. The Winchester branch bay is seen on the right.

Author's collection

Lords and gentry of the area, together with their money, which influenced its final construction, as opposed to most other railway projects, which floundered through their embryo stages because of opposition from the very same classes.

By this time most of the railways in the country had been completed, criss-crossing in all directions, making the new crossroads at Didcot more effective by making it possible to reach all parts of the country.

In May 1885 the Newbury end of the line was connected to the GWR main line which ran from Paddington via Reading as far as Hungerford. A junction was made at Enborne, about one mile from Newbury station to connect with the now completed southern section through to Winchester, and via the LSWR to Southampton, and furthermore connected to Portsmouth, reflecting the original dreams which prompted the proposals for such a line.

This line never really reached its ideals. The through trunk road, which was the main object, having ended up as only a single line, did not carry the traffic hoped for, and therefore developed into no more than branch line status with a sparse service. The cost of construction was very high, followed by less than expected income.

Probably the largest single factor was brought about by the intervention of the GWR. In their arrangements to assist in building the line, and later agreeing to operate it, they imposed such stringent restrictions, such as taking more than fifty per cent of the revenue, and forcing an agreement that they need only run a service on a regular basis as necessary. Their justification for this was that their contribution towards the construction costs warranted it. More to the point, and believed by some, was the fact that the GWR had already got the bulk of the traffic which could possibly use the line. If that was so, why should they consider using this line at the expense of their own railway?

It has been suggested that the object of working the line with these stringent limitations was mainly to prevent others from doing so, thus preserving their own interests. Whatever the reasons, the line was condemned to that of a rural branch.

The Didcot to Newbury section became the most viable because it joined these two towns together in trade, and at the same time provided communication for the intermediate communities.

At Didcot a separate bay line was provided for the branch trains at the east end, also the crossover structure allowed for trains to leave the branch to run into the station or run via the avoiding line direct towards the north.

During 1885, after the Newbury line was opened, Didcot station underwent some considerable changes. The original Brunel all-over roof was demolished and the platforms were each fitted with a standard type canopy.

4-4-0 No.3254 with a train of clerestory coaches on the DN&S at Winchester heading towards Didcot. *Author's collection*

Unfortunately, the old etching of the station (see Chapter Five) is all we have to tell us what it was like. This drawing shows the Brunel roof with its elevated ventilators over the running lines. Another artist shows the station with an apex roof when depicting the arrival of the first train from Newbury, only three years prior to the new canopies being fitted. It seems that the artist has used a little license; this type of roof was never in use.

An official GWR plan of Didcot by Brunel of the station layout dated 1851 – showing suggested alterations – is very interesting. There is no doubt that at this time the station was completely covered as described by Ernest Struggles. What is most interesting about this Brunel drawing is the items not described by Ernest, probably because they had never been carried out. The plan appears to be for proposals for alterations to the station and also to the track layout; proposals which failed to materialise.

On each of the four roads is shown a carriage or wagon turntable just a little way inside the station at the western end. Each of these tables had a connecting line across to the next one, allowing vehicles to be detached from one train and then to be manhandled across to another line to connect with another service. The wealthy people of the day, wishing to transport their own horse-drawn carriages with them, were the only ones likely to be able to take advantage of this facility. It is also noted that private horse-drawn carriages influenced the design of the first private railway saloon coaches.

It seems that this proposal was never followed up. I'm sure that Ernest Struggles would have made fair comment if it had been, he would have been scathing about the inconvenience to the passengers, having to negotiate the dangers of the turntable wells, each of which had two steps down from each side.

In addition to these four small turntables there was also a larger one located outside the east end on the nearside line (now the down main line) possibly for the use of engines, to save the tiresome trip across all the junctions to the loco shed. Another small turntable is also shown on a spur backing off this same line, this one is specifically intended for turning wagons on to either of the three short sidings used by local traders.

This plan also showed another proposed alteration which was never carried out. From a point on the Oxford junction, starting about two hundred yards from the station, a line was proposed to run behind the station, using two of the yard roads, and to rejoin the line at the east end just beyond the end of the platform, to operate as an avoiding line.

The most probable reason for not continuing with these alterations was that the more effective avoiding line was laid from East junction to North junction in 1856.

When E.T. MacDermot referred to the opening of the Oxford line he stated:

...on the same day a large junction station was opened at Didcot, consisting of four lines and five very narrow platforms, under an 'all-over' roof, which did duty until *burnt down some forty years later.* A footnote reads, *On the 11th March 1885.* It was an error on his part, that was the year in which the station was rebuilt, it was in fact the same date one year later when the fire occurred.

A local fire officer, L. Didcock, related to me how the fire was discovered at midday. Didcot had no fire service at the time so the nearest firemen and appliance was called from Harwell, some three miles away. It duly arrived with its horse-drawn steam pump but soon realised that the conflagration was far too serious to tackle alone, the wooden buildings were well alight.

A call made to Oxford on the railway telegraph system was received at a very opportune moment. It transpired that the Oxford pump – one of a similar type – had been to a function to give a display of its efficiency, and at that time had just returned to Oxford on a flat railway wagon. At this time the wagon was attached to a locomotive and being propelled into the dock for unloading. The order was given for the engine to take the appliance directly to Didcot on the wagon.

The journey took eighteen minutes for the ten miles, with the men riding on the wagon preparing their engine, raising steam to enable them to start pumping immediately on arrival.

The Oxford Volunteer Fire Brigade records show the following entry for 1886:

Didcot Station, Great Western Railway. 'Call received at 1.30 and steamer at work at Didcot (a distance of ten miles) at 2 o'clock.'

The results of the fire were disastrous, as the pictures show. One feature is prominent – the fireplace, still standing in the remains of the wall, is most likely to have been the seat of the fire.

On 13 March 1886 the *Oxford Times* comprehensively covered the incident, some extracts of which are included here:

A most destructive fire broke out last Thursday afternoon, a few minutes before one o'clock. The work at the station was proceeding as usual, when the clerk at the bookstall, and one of the inspectors, noticed more than the ordinary quantity of smoke on the platform... it appears to have been in the telegraph office that the fire originated, but from what cause has not been ascertained... the station master and inspectors with great promptness set to work organising the men, but it was soon seen that their efforts would be useless. Meanwhile a message had been sent to Oxford by telegram, and in a short time the splendid fire engine was brought down the line and immediately set to work. Subsequently there came the fire engines from Wallingford and Abingdon.

Telegraph communication was stopped early by the snapping of the wires. The goods service was at once suspended, but the passenger traffic was not much interfered with, owing to the company being able to use their excellent loop-line.

The fire continued with unabated force until evening. The principal building was a substantial structure, built

The forecourt of the station after the fire of 1886. Note the children of the day in their costumes. *L Didcock collection*

The burned out buildings and down main line platform looking west. The fireplace in the ruins of the office building is where the fire is reputed to have started. *L Didcock collection*

The true devastation to the station is seen in this picture looking across from the platform to the buildings across the road.

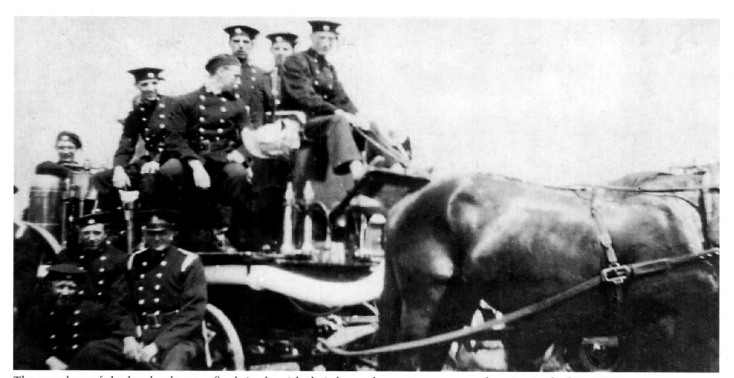

The members of the local volunteer fire brigade with their horse-drawn steam powered engine in the late 1880s.

Author's collection

The Didcot station staff in 1886 soon after the station was rebuilt following the fire. Note the new fire office and the rows of fire buckets suspended from the roof!

Oxford County Libraries (Didcot)

about forty years ago of bricks and masonry, the timbers being of pitch pine. . . the flames spreading the opposite way caught the slight buildings on the other side, and the various waiting and refreshment rooms were destroyed. These buildings were only erected last year.

A codicil to this report said:

The fire originated in this manner; An employee was holding an oil lamp in front of the fire in one of the waiting rooms, when he accidentally spilled some oil. The fire rapidly ignited it, and before he had time to take any action, the flames were roaring up the chimney. The chimney caught fire, and it ran up through the telegraph office where the fire broke out. The news created quite a sensation in Wallingford, Abingdon, Oxford, and through the district; and about four o'clock there were several hundred persons at Didcot. The flames could be seen for miles around.

The devastation was terrific, but with the enormous work force available in those times the rebuilding was completed within a few months.

Following this the station settled down to running a regular service, with mixed or standard gauge throughout the area; there were few complications with traffic.

Through trains could now run from London to the west, and also from south to north, in fact, realising some of Brunel's ambitions. Timetables were issued monthly under the authority of the company and issued free to the gentry and such like. One timetable issued in 1886 covered the services on the whole of the GWR system, including the railway boat services. A typical service from this timetable is the one starting from Paddington at 10am, Oxford 11.50am, (travel from Reading and Didcot to change at Oxford), Worcester 2.5pm, Stourbridge 3.10pm, Wolverhampton 4.5pm, Shrewsbury 5.18pm, Birkenhead 7.40pm, Manchester 8.55pm. Change at Manchester for Liverpool.

A sample of fares from the same timetable for services from Didcot to London:

	1st	2nd	3rd
Express trains	11s 3d	8s 2d	–
Ordinary trains	9s 4d	7s 0d	4s 5d

(Third class represents exactly one penny per mile)

Excursions advertised:
Paddington to Windsor & back   2s 6d
Paddington to Taplow & back   2s 6d
Paddington to Henley & back   3s 0d

These particular stations had become favourite picnic places by the river, prompting the railway to offer cheaper fares and stating 'All in third class covered coaches.'

During this same period the railway slowly developed its running roads in the Didcot area. Traffic had increased, extra lines were needed to cope with it. On 12 April 1890 the GWR sent a letter to the Board of Trade (BOT) who, at that time, were responsible for overseeing all new work carried out by the railways. In the letter they referred to

the new goods line which had just been completed from Didcot as far as Moreton Cutting, stating that it was ready for inspection. It was duly inspected by BOT Inspector Col. Rich on 19 April 1890, after which he sent the following report:

I have the honour to report for the information of the Board of Trade that in compliance with the instructions in your minute of the 14th inst. I have inspected the new junctions between the Great Western main lines from Oxford, and from Bristol, and a new up goods relief line which has been constructed at the east end of Didcot station.

A new cabin has been built. It contains 27 working levers plus two spare levers and is named East junction Cabin.

When number five signal is lowered for a main line train it should lock number six point lever.

Subject to this alteration being made, I can recommend the Board of Trade to approve of these new works. The new relief line is only intended for goods at present.

In the same year the railway also asked the BOT to inspect the provision of a new siding for the accommodation of traffic to and from Mr Rich's works at that place. This was to be worked by key on train staff on the single line from Didcot to Upton, spring points and disc to be worked from the ground frame.

On 17 November 1892 the railway requested inspection of the new relief line from Didcot to Cholsey. There is no record of inspection, but it was opened for the four and half miles to the new Cholsey station, for the use of goods traffic only in November, and for passenger trains on 27 December. This particular section was part of the quadrupling from Paddington to Didcot.

An up goods loop was proposed between North junction and East junction in March 1901, completed seven months later, and passed by Major Pringle for use on 13 November 1901.

Summary of tickets issued at Didcot							
	February 1889				July 1889		
		£	s	d		£	s	d
First Single	25	10	1	1	32	6	19	5
Second Single	42½	5	13	0½	56	15	7	11
Third Single	323	15	5	11	565	45	4	0
Party Single	1097½	90	9	11	1787½	174	18	7
First Return	8	2	18	0	16	8	7	4
Second Return	48	15	12	10	106	38	18	9
Third Return	24	2	6	10	20	2	5	3
Parliamentary	247½	19	10	2½	176½	22	7	6
Market tickets	30	3	12	6	23	2	15	7
Excursions	15½	2	6	11	59	15	0	0
Excess		5	12	0		7	16	11
	1761	173	10	10				
Season					1		6	9
Picnic					29	3	10	1
Paris Exhibition					1	2	2	3
					2872	346	2	3

First entry of season tickets   1st July 1889
First entry of printed tickets   7th July 1889

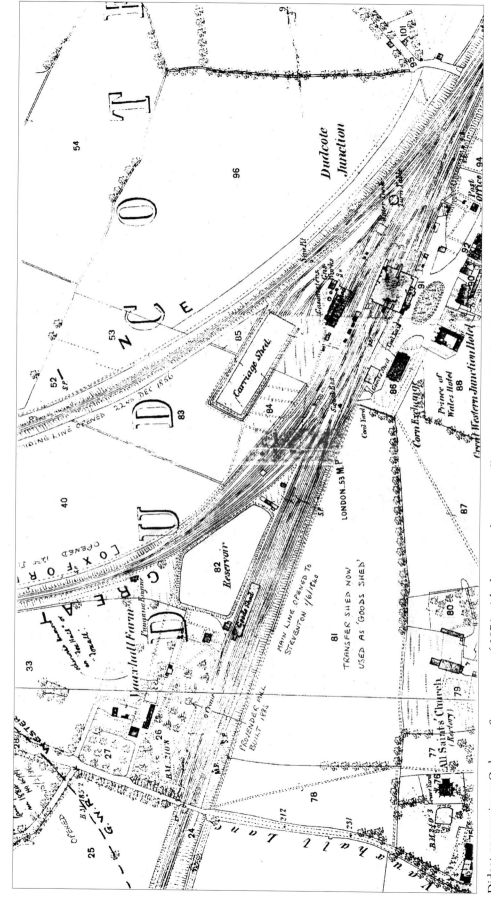

Didcot as seen in an Ordnance Survey map of 1874 with the covered station still in existence, and before the provender mill was built.

CHAPTER SEVEN

Signalling

When the Great Western Railway was first built there were no thoughts of having signalmen to control the movement of trains, but by the time the line had reached Didcot and beyond, some measure of control had been instigated. From the outset it had been considered that the company's policemen posted at level crossings and stations or patrolling their beats, would be able to control the traffic by hand signals, just as the 'Metropolitan police did on the streets of London.'

For the first few months they had no means of giving signals after dark. On 24 August 1838 the London committee ordered 'Lamps for the Police' and at the same time asked for 'police boxes'; when supplied, these wooden sentry type boxes were just large enough for a man to stand up in, furnished only with a small seat but no door or heating. At first they were placed in a fixed position, but very soon afterwards they were made to pivot in order that they could be rotated to turn their backs to the weather.

Although the London committee suggested police boxes in 1838, several years must have elapsed before they were commonplace, as the following letter confirms. Written in 1840 it shows disgust at the removal of a hut which the policemen had erected for themselves at Basildon, ten or so miles to the east of Didcot.

From the Reverend R.R. Fisher, Basildon Vicarage, 26 November 1840:

I am requested by several of my parishoners from feelings of sympathy, most respectfully to represent to the Directors of the railway the present pitiable situation of the policemen who are stationed at the lane leading to the Church of this Parish, in consequence of the removal of a kind of hut which they had erected near the gates. The situation is exposed to a strong current of wind when it blows from the north, and is sufficiently near the Thames to be subject to the fogs. In this situation according to your regulations, a poor man is isolated for eleven hours, without the possibility of approaching a fire or procuring any warm refreshments thro' the night. I need not represent to you the misery of such circumstances, or of the almost certain consequences of the good health; but perhaps you are not aware that in the case of sudden illness, or the drowsy effects of intense cold, no other person would be at hand to prevent any accident to a passing train. The present policemen have by their civility
and uniform attention procured the favourable regard of all the inhabitants of the district, and I cannot but think that the most effectual means of obtaining a respectful body of policemen, is to extend to them every accommodation and comfort of which their situation is capable, consistent with the rigid discipline which is necessary for the security of the public.

Until the advent of the fixed signal boxes and locking gear those little boxes were the only means of shelter. At this time, the only need for policemen was to control traffic mainly at stations and level crossings. For example, the long section between Wallingford Road and Steventon, out in the country as it were, was in the sole hands of the driver with perhaps a patrolling policeman here and there; the village of Didcot was not yet on the railway map.

By the time Didcot station was built with its rather complex layout of points and crossovers the need for organised control was much greater. Definite information on the original arrangements is somewhat lacking but it can be safely assumed that several policemen would have been needed to operate the numerous points and to give signals to the drivers. Just when mechanical indication was installed at Didcot is uncertain but from other sources it can be deduced that it was most likely to have been in operation from the opening of the station. Soon after the opening of the line as far as Twyford in 1839 a notice was issued to drivers:

Notice to Enginemen

On and after the first of July the 10 o'clock morning and the 6 o'clock evening Twyford trains will not call at Maidenhead up or down. The down trains will pass through the shed without going into the siding. The attention of the enginemen is called to a signal, applied to the lever of the switches, to denote whether they be open or shut. Two targets are so attached so that if both is seen the switch is open, but if both range in a line so that only one is seen the switch is right for the straight line. Before coming to the shed in either direction the steam must be shut off at a sufficient distance to allow the engine to be perfectly in command and able to be stopped in case anything is wrong.

Paddington. 26th July 1839.
Seymour Clarke Chief Superintendent.
(The shed mentioned refers to the covered station)

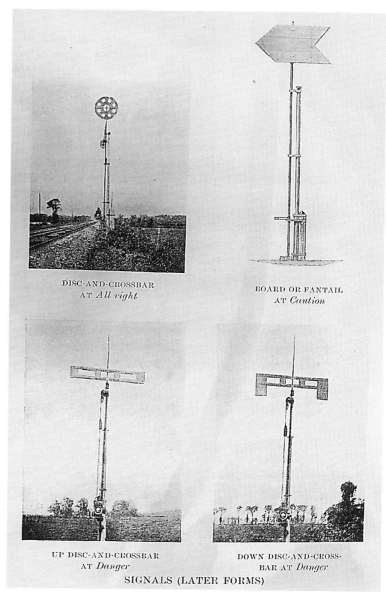

DISC-AND-CROSSBAR
AT *All right*

BOARD OR FANTAIL
AT *Caution*

UP DISC-AND-CROSSBAR
AT *Danger*

DOWN DISC-AND-CROSS-
BAR AT *Danger*

SIGNALS (LATER FORMS)

Above left: A sketch of the original police box showing open front and small seat. **Above right:** The types of signals by Brunel which he claimed to be more efficient by being able to give both stop and proceed indications. *MacDermot's History*

It is interesting to note that this notice was not posted until nearly a month after its authorisation. One can only wonder what confusion reigned in this period!

Only the best of policemen were selected to operate these switches and were called 'switchmen' to distinguish them from 'common constables'. For this, they received higher pay, and a bonus for good conduct. An official statement on the activities of switchmen and policemen issued in 1839 is: 'The policemen make signals with their arms; by this the enginemen are principally governed.' From this statement it is apparent that there were no fixed signals of any sort for more than a year after the opening of the railway. By the same token it becomes almost certain that by the time Didcot station was opened some

five years later there must have been some kind of mechanical signalling, but exactly what type is not certain. From other factors, the signals would most likely have been the 'disc and crossbar' type, with discs on the appropriate point levers, similar to those described in use at Maidenhead.

During this period Brunel was experimenting with various means of indicating the position of the points. One of his designs for operating the points and at the same time indicating their position was called a 'capstan'. These came into use towards the end of the same year. A firm, Slaughter and Company, of Bristol supplied 'Sets of switches complete with capstans, disc and quadrant' for £50 each.

The disc or targets when set to face the driver indicated the points were set for the main line, but were turned edgeways for the siding. For this particular purpose they became standard on the Great Western, also on Brunel's other railways until after 1885. Therefore this type also become a possibility for use at Didcot in the early days.

The earliest mention of fixed signals is found in Gooch's *Regulations for the working of engines and trains on and after 30th March 1840*, issued for the opening to Reading on that day. This document gives the daily working of the various engines, and concludes:

A signal ball will be seen at the entrance to Reading station when the line is right for the train to go in. If the ball is not visible then the train must not pass it.

A somewhat vague instruction but more were to follow. In 1874 a Mr Rapier in writing about the railways said:

Fixed signals at Reading. On the Great Western Railway was introduced about 1839. The ball drawn up to the top of the mast, after the manner of a high water signal, indicated 'safety' and a common stable lamp was hooked on at night instead of the ball.

There seems to be no other confirmation regarding the lantern. This type of signal had a very short life, in 1843 suggestions were made for the general use of a new type of signal which Brunel had invented. The General Traffic Committee had a meeting in 1840 from which the following extracts are taken:

November 18th – Switchman at Slough dismissed for failing to lower his signal – (All clear signal left showing behind a train).

December 9th – Engineman fined for passing Southall with a red light shown to him and the station signal also being down at the time – (Signal at danger).

Brunel was dubious about issuing notices to enginemen. He told the Select Committee in 1841 that 'The best of them could neither read nor write.'

By this time Brunel's new type of signal was superseding the ground discs, they were more efficient both for use as main line signals and more importantly for indicating a definite stop or proceed signal.

This new signal, known as the disc-and-crossbar remained in service for many years and as such it can be assumed that this type of signal would have been in use from the time of Didcot station opening. Unfortunately the only picture of Didcot in its early days does not show any signals or even a policeman. There were certainly some signals in the 1860s because Mr Struggles wrote of them but that was twenty years later.

The signal consisted of a tall mast with a large disc at the top to show 'All right' and a crossbar immediately below the disc at right angles to indicate 'Stop'. When the disc faced the driver the bar was then in line along the track and not seen by the driver and he was permitted to pass it, but when the post had been rotated so that the crossbar faced the driver, he must stop. At a later date instead of rotating the whole of the post which was very cumbersome, the main part of it was firmly positioned in the ground, and only the top section with signals attached was turned to show the necessary signal. In addition the top of the fixed portion was able to be anchored to the ground with stays to make it more secure. Some of these signals were as tall as sixty feet and caught the high winds. To ease the wind pressure Brunel had holes cut into the signals. These signals were considered by Brunel to be a great improvement on the signals used by other railways because of their ability to give a positive stop or proceed indication. They did however have one failing, they were not able to give a caution signal.

Brunel was very concerned that a caution signal should be given and designed what he called a 'flag' signal in the shape of a fan which could be opened and closed by the use of cords and pulleys. Officially these signals were known as 'Flag Signals', but to the men as 'Fantails' or 'Kites'. Their life was short due to the type of material being used, and not strong enough to stand up to the strong winds; one of Brunel's rare failures! Besides this problem the policemen operating these were required to signal drivers with a lamp at night. Again it is not known for certain whether any of these were in use at Didcot, possibly they were used in conjunction with the disc-and-crossbar.

Although Brunel had stated his opinion as to the literacy of the drivers, the traffic department issued regulations in 1841 under the heading 'Line Signals' together with drawings of policemen, describing the hand signals they should use, and giving instructions for the use of hand lamps at night. The instructions read:

Stations, Tunnels, and Gate Signals.

Signals by means of a round disc and crossbar on a mast, also by flags in the daytime and lights at night on a separate flagstaff, are provided at each station, at the entrance to long tunnels, and at all gates which shut across the line, to be used for the purpose to be described. The crossbar when seen along the line is the signal to STOP. The red flag on the flagstaff by day and the red light by dusk and at night, is also the DANGER signal to STOP, and must be shown in every instance of the line being obstructed, or of any accident or stoppage at a station, in tunnels, or on the line, and also after the passage of any train or engine in the same direction along the line. The green flag on the flagstaff by day, and the green light by night, is the CAUTION signal to slacken speed, and must be shown, after three minutes, until ten minutes shall have elapsed from the passing of a train or engine in the same direction, as well as in any case where it may seem proper to recommend a reduced speed.

The disc shown along the line implies 'All Right'. The white light at night also implied 'All Right'. The disc must always be reversed (so as not to be seen along the railway) and the crossbar must be shown whenever the DANGER is indicated upon either flagstaff, whether by red flag or red light; and consequently the full disc will only be seen when the line is perfectly clear and no engine or train have passed for three minutes previously.

The flagstaff to show signals on the down line is always on the south and left hand side of the down train; and for the up line is always on the north and left-hand side of the a train; but when necessary to give a Caution or Danger signals to the engine in each direction, the flags and lights must be shown on both flagstaffs at the same time as well as by crossbar. In the case of fog, both the day and night signals must be shown simultaneously.

Brunel seemed to be very pleased with his new signals, saying:

They were very much improved in construction, and the code and mode of signalling was also greatly improved. The flags used for caution in conjunction with the disc and crossbar made for greater safety.

The success of these signals ended the use of the dubious 'fantails', particularly in the view of the superintendent of the Bristol area, Mr Frederick Clarke, when he wrote to the General Manager on 19th October of that year:

The consumption of flags on the Exeter line is enormous. The flags will not stand a week. These last few windy days have, I believe, put every flag on the line out of repair. They are flying from the masthead in streamers. Two of the large masts (disc and crossbar) have also been blown down.

As a result of this and no doubt many other complaints, the Traffic Committee ordered on 27th October:

...new signals in tin, corrugated iron, or wood to be substituted for the present flags on account of the expense in constant repairs as well as the difficulty in keeping them on the staff in tempestuous weather, at a cost estimated by Brunel to be £2.10 shillings each.

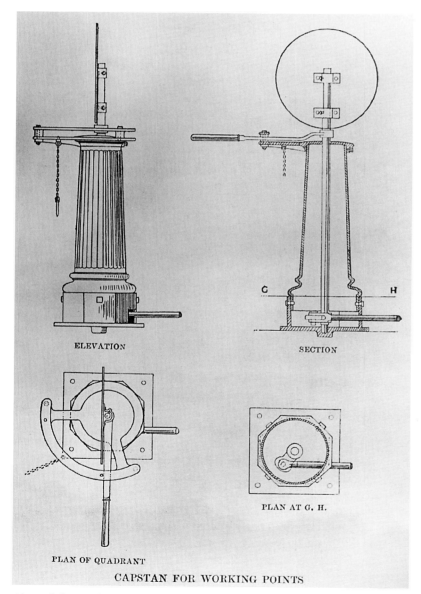

ELEVATION

SECTION

PLAN AT G. H.

PLAN OF QUADRANT

CAPSTAN FOR WORKING POINTS

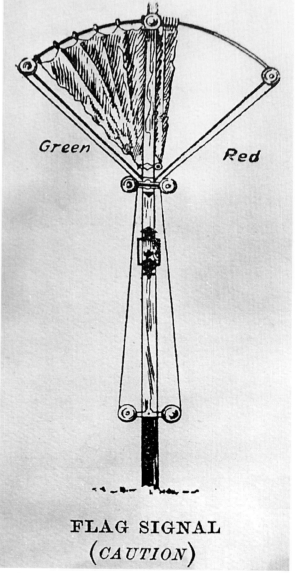

Green

Red

FLAG SIGNAL
(*CAUTION*)

Above left: An illustration of 'Capstans' designed by Brunel for policemen to operate points and simultaneously give an indication to the driver regarding their position. **Above right:** A sketch of a flag signal indicating the operation of the separate flags. Designed by Brunel to be used as caution when the green flag was showing.

MacDermot's History

This led to an arrow shaped wooden board being designed and put into use, it being red on one side and green on the other, on a revolving post, to take the place of the double flags. Like the previous ones they were also sighted on the left-hand side of the line to which they applied. The red side when turned on pointed towards the line to which it applied and the green side away from it; All Right being shown by the main signal. They were first established in 1842 soon after the previous notice was issued and remained in use for some thirty years. The lamps of the unused flagstaffs were now put to use at these signals and erected on a separate staff. These dates and instructions confirm that Didcot had good signals right from the start.

To enable Mr Saunders to reply to enquiries made by the Railway Commissioners as to the visibility of the signal lights, Gooch wrote to him in 1848:

The station signal lights are of the most powerful we have and are made with argon burners one inch in diameter. These lights may be seen in a clear night several miles distant. We have in fact no straight line of sufficient length for the distance to prevent us from seeing the lights. Our Twyford signals are seen quite clearly from a distance of between four and five miles. I cannot say what the comparative distances at which the various colours in use may be seen but the order in which they may be stated is as follows – 1st White, 2nd Red, 3rd Green. I think red and green are the best colours to use for colour lights as producing the greatest contrast with each other and with white. In thick or foggy weather the distance the lights are seen depends entirely on the density of the fog. I have known it so bad that they could not be seen until within a few yards of them. There is also a difficulty in fog in distinguishing at a distance a white light from a red one. The fog gives the white light a red appearance.

From these quotations one can conclude that right from the start Didcot had some sort of fixed signals, assuming by the dates of instruction that there would be disc-and-crossbar as main signals and arrow boards to act as distant signals. In early references to disc-and-crossbar signals it states that 'there was only need to have one at each end of road stations.' These stations referred to in this manner being the ones located near to main roads which crossed the railway, such as Steventon.

The 'mode of signalling' referred to by Brunel in conjunction with his new type of signal was the Time Interval System, which had been in operation from the opening of the line, but which had been improved by the introduction of rules governing its use. An electric telegraph system was installed for the working of Box Tunnel as early as December 1847 but failed to meet expectations, becoming a total failure after only two years and several years elapsed before it was again workable.

On the other hand, trains were being worked from Paddington to Twyford by the electric telegraph from 1861, but only as a means of sending forward the information as to which train was on line and the time of departure. Time

intervals governing the use of signals remained:

...three minutes Danger followed by seven minutes Caution after the passage of any train until 1852, when they were altered to five minutes Danger and five more for Caution after a passenger, and eight minutes Danger and seven more for Caution after a goods train. After the whole ten minutes, or fifteen, as the case may be, had elapsed, the signals were restored to their normal position of All Right, provided no obstruction existed within the sight of the signalman except at certain stations; Slough, Reading, Didcot, Swindon, Bath, Gloucester, and all junctions and terminal stations, where the normal position was Danger, only altered to admit a train.

These intervals remained until 1887. The sensible distinction between passenger trains and goods trains was particular to the Great Western; on other railways the intervals were five minutes Danger and five minutes Caution for all trains.

Whether the policemen were issued with watches or note books is not recorded, or whether they had to rely on their own judgement of time, and memory.

The duties of the police are described in the rules dated 1841:

The duties of the police may be stated generally to consist in the preservation of order in the stations and on the line of the railway. They are to give and receive signals; to keep the lines free from casual and wilful obstructions; to assist in cases of accidents; to caution strangers of danger on the railways; to remove intruders of all descriptions, to give notice of arrivals and departures; to watch movements of embankments and cuttings; to inspect the rails and solidity of timbers; to guard and watch the companies premises; and to convey the earliest information on every subject to their appointed station or superior officer.

Quite a considerable amount of responsibility was placed on the shoulders of the policemen, and it stayed this way until the advent of signal cabins.

In February of 1852 a meeting was held with The Electric Telegraph Company. That company was to lay and maintain wires on the Great Western lines, charging an annual rent for their use and giving the railway company the option to purchase. The Bristol & Exeter Railway having made a similar agreement and the telegraph already being in use on the South Devon, its completion between London and Plymouth was thus ensured. The wires were already up as far as Reading; they reached Bristol in May and were completed to Exeter in August. By the end of the year almost the whole of the Great Western was completed.

Didcot therefore had the benefit of electric telegraph working during the first half of 1852 in conjunction with time interval working.

MacDermot's History gives details of early block telegraph working. The details are rather vague as to the mode of signalling on the main line prior to 1873. One gets the impression that Didcot was still worked by the time interval system. The block telegraph was in use between Paddington and Ealing by 1867. The system was extended from Ealing to Southall in 1871 and Maidenhead was reached by the end of the next year. The text continues:

...and by Christmas 1873 the gaps between Maidenhead and Pangbourne and Goring and Thingley were filled, completing the block telegraph between London and Bristol.

However, a meeting was held at Paddington on 27 January 1871, attended by representatives from each division with Mr Grierson in the Chair. The object of the meeting was to discuss the block telegraph system now in force on the line, and to decide upon standard regulations for working under each system in the future. Should line clear be given when the train arrived within the home signal or when the station was clear? The general consensus was, line clear should be returned when the train had arrived within the home signal, but each divisional manager outlined specific locations where the station should be clear before line clear was returned. Mr Stevens representing the Reading division was of the opinion that line clear should not be returned until the station was clear excepting at Reading, Didcot and Oxford. Unfortunately there isn't any reference to the system in force at that time. If the time interval system was still in force then a train would be allowed to approach even if the station was blocked.

An appendix to the minutes entitled *'List of Portions of the Line worked by Block Telegraph, January 1871'* lists Goring to Pangbourne on the up line only as being worked under the telegraph system. Spagnoletti's disc was in use and instructions on how the section between Pangbourne and Goring was worked were dated 8 May 1865.

There was also a 'list of signals which work to CAUTION and DANGER only, and whether or not the superintendents recommend that they should be made to show ALL RIGHT.'

As far as Didcot was concerned the signals in question were as follows:

Station	Signals	To show All Right or not
Didcot East Junc	All Up Signals	Yes
Didcot East Junc	All Down Signals	No
Didcot North Junc	All Up Signals	No
Didcot North Junc	All Down Signals	Yes
Didcot West Junc	Double Branch Signals up and down	No
Didcot Main Line	Down Main and up and Down Auxillary	Yes
Didcot West Junc	Up Home	No

At that time there appears to have been three different systems for absolute block working on the Great Western Railway, namely Spagnoletti's Disc Block Instrument, Tyer's Block Signalling Instruments and the Single Needle Instruments with and without bells.

There had been no real improvement in signalling since the early days until the disc-and-crossbars, together with their subsidiary fantails, were replaced by semaphores, the first of these being between Paddington and Kensal Green on 1 April 1865. Elsewhere the disc-and-crossbar were still in use until November 1869, when the gradual substitution of semaphores 'wherever practicable' was ordered and they ceased to be made.

The early semaphores were constructed with a slot in the post for the signal arm to drop into when it indicated clear, and out of sight; danger being shown by the arm at the horizontal position, caution was indicated by the arm in the half-way position. In 1873 the caution position was abandoned and the all right signal defined by the arm hanging down the post.

The distinction of a distant signal by means of a notch cut in the end of the arm was adopted in 1876. Semaphores with the arm outside the post began to appear at about the same time. The GWR design of semaphore was evolved about 1887 and was considered to be the best proportioned railway signal in the country.

Disc-and-crossbar signals remained in use at many locations, often intermixed with semaphores, throughout the 'seventies and early 'eighties, but few survived after 1890.

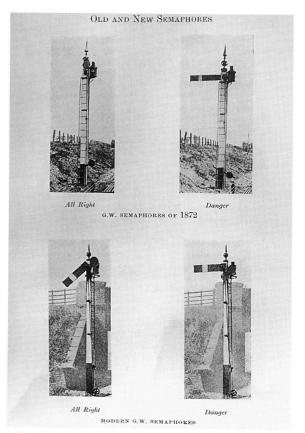

OLD AND NEW SEMAPHORES

All Right   *Danger*

G.W. SEMAPHORES OF 1872

All Right   *Danger*

MODERN G.W. SEMAPHORES

Old and new types of semaphore signals. The top left signal has dropped into a slot in the post to indicate 'Clear'.
MacDermot's History

The signal boxes in the Didcot area have had varying lives, being built, rebuilt and moved to different locations, some only a few yards and others further away. As far as is known the table below gives the dates of opening and closure of each of them.

To advance with the times, the Great Western made a bold move and built a new signal box at Didcot North junction to be worked completely by electrical equipment. At the time the *Great Western Railway Magazine* carried a comprehensive article headed:

THE FIRST GREAT WESTERN
ELECTRIC SIGNALLING INSTALLATION

In our May issue of 1904, the announcement was made that the directors had authorised the installation of an electrical power system of working points and signals at Didcot. This was completed and brought into use on 16th ult., and is giving entire satisfaction. A new signal box has been built midway between the former North Junction and West Curve signal boxes, and all points and signals hitherto worked from those boxes are now operated from the new one.

The signalman is provided with a means of easily moving the points and signals by the aid of electricity, compressed air or other motive agency, thus being relieved of all manual labour. It is still necessary to have a locking frame in a signal box, with signals interlocked with each other and connections between the box and the various points and signals.

An advantage is that the BOT permit facing points to be worked by power systems at a distance of 300 yards from the controlling lever, whereas the manual system, the distance is only 200 yards.

The system adopted at Didcot is an all electric one, by Messrs. Siemens Bros. and Company, Ltd., of London, the points and signals being moved by small motors, by a current of 120 volts. A pair of points of the heaviest section (92 to 100 lbs per yard) uses only two to four amps, the movement taking 2 to 3 seconds. The mechanical locking is a special feature of Messrs Siemens system; preventing one or several signals being used

a second time until another has been replaced.

Any number of points can be moved as quickly as the signalman can do so, the motors working practically simultaneously, but perfect safety is secured by ensuring that all points have moved correctly before a signal be lowered. The time occupied is no longer than a manual frame; in fact, it is shorter, as only one lever is used for both points and lock. Indeed, we may add that in a recent test at Didcot seven sets of points and four fouling bars were operated in 6 seconds.

When the control contacts are closed, the indicator gives the proper indication, i.e.'normal' or 'reverse' in the case of points, and in the case of signals 'on' or 'off'.

The signals are operated by motors in a similar manner to the points, but there is an electrical coupling or 'slot' between the motor and the signal arm. In the case of several signals on a gantry, only one motor is required with as many couplings as there are arms to be worked. The arm of which ever the coupling magnet is energised moves only with the motor, all the other arms being locked.

The electric is obtained from accumulators placed in a special building adjacent to the signal box. These are charged from the Locomotive Department electrical power installation at the Didcot Provender Stores.

The installation has been made under the supervision of the company's Signal Engineer A. T. Blackall. The general scheme having been prepared by him in conjunction with W.E. Scourfield, his principle assistant.

The signal box remained in use until the closure of all signal boxes in the area in 1965. It reverted to manual operation during 1936, although there is a record of £1,800 being spent on 'Renewals of signalling arrangements' on 17 December 1925.

The cost of Siemens Bros. contract for the new signal box was £2,675. Additional cost to the company was £675.

This electric box was considered to be a great advance to modern signalling, operating the most up to date points and signals.

Name of Box	Opened		Closed	Levers	
Didcot East Junction	1	22-12-1856	c.4-1890		
	2	c.4-1890	23-10-1932	45	
	3	23-10-1932	17-5-1965	150	
Didcot East End	By 1874		23-10-1932	57	New frame c.1905
Didcot West End	1				
	2		c.1932	51	New frame c.1904
	3	c.9-1932	17-5-1965	88	vt 5 bar frame
Didcot Foxhall Junction	1	By 1874	27-11-1915	25	New Stud frame 1907
	2	27-11-1915	13-10-1931	45	vt 3 bar frame
	3	13-10-1931	17-5-1965	76	vt 5 bar frame
Didcot North Junction	Cabin				
	1	22-12-1856	16-7-1905		
	2	16-7-1905		38	Siemens power frame
				36	Mechanical frame 1936
			17-5-1965	89	Box extended 1941 with 5 bar locking installed 28-6-1941
Didcot West Curve	1886		16-7-1905		Work taken over by Didcot North

Left: The electrical equipment attached to the up junction signal post at Didcot North. Note the number of rods travelling up the post to operate the five signals.

Below left: The new signal box at Didcot North junction, built in 1904 to house the latest electrical equipment. The lower building housed the accumulators to operate the points and signals. This building survived as the platelayers cabin when the box reverted to manual operation.

Below right: The down starting signal towards Appleford. The counter balance weight can be seen at the top of the post by the signal arm.
Mrs E Rice

CHAPTER EIGHT

The Provender Stores

The Horse Provender Stores, Didcot

An unusual view of the provender stores across the reservoir showing the three signals controlling movements on the three roads.
Author's collection

The Great Western Railway was without doubt one of the country's biggest employers of horses during the late nineteenth century and some way beyond. Throughout the whole of the system the GWR had developed a comprehensive cartage operation for collection and delivery of goods at almost all stations. The numerous horses required to carry out the task presented a huge logistics problem in supplying foodstuffs and bedding materials.

In preference to relying on local farmers to supply these requirements on an individual basis to the stations, and therefore having no overall control over the quality supplied, the GWR built a depot at Handsworth in Birmingham to provide uniformity and ensure regular supplies.

When the horse population grew to reach three thousand or so the depot was too small to cope with the storage and milling. In addition, the distribution to all parts of the railway was far too wide ranging, London in the east, Penzance to the west, with Wales as an added problem. It seems to have been an ill founded site.

The need came to select a more central site. Didcot had always been regarded as central; so where better? It was well placed, in a position to collect and distribute to all parts, benefiting also from the newly opened Newbury & Southampton line.

An additional consideration in siting the stores at Didcot was the fact that at the time, with local traffic not being in abundance, there was ample room, not only for the buildings, but plenty of yard space for receiving wagons.

In 1885 this huge provender store was opened; situated to the west of the station on the northern side of the line, a stark looking building dominating the skyline. The building was of a very sturdy structure, encompassing a steel girder framework, rising to a mean height of 66ft. The length of the main building was 205ft by 49ft wide. There were four floors constructed with solid timber to withstand the weight of the exceptionally heavy machinery which was to be employed.

Inside, three rail lines ran the entire length of the building. Two spiral staircases 4ft in diameter with cast-iron treads and risers with wrought iron handrails supported by ornamental balusters rose 45ft to the top floor.

The superintendent had an office inside which measured 14ft by 15ft, whilst the several clerks were cramped into their office of 17ft by 13ft.

The building had two water towers built in brick rising to 74ft and 88ft respectively, each carrying a steel tank measuring 23ft by 18ft 6in and 7ft high. Water to supply the mill and the surrounding premises was pumped into these tanks by a steam-driven pump, operated from the adjoining boiler house.

To maintain a constant supply, a reservoir was made in the junction at the west end of the station by the damming of the hollow, later this was made deeper by raising the height of the dam. In later years water was pumped from a well sunk in the railway property close to where the railway crossed the Thames near Appleford, to maintain the reservoir. To save paying the Thames Commissioners for water it was a common practice to sink a well on railway property, knowing that it would fill in from the river; with this ploy no charge could be made.

The water in the tanks at this great height was fed by gravity to the station, yards, and to the elevated tank in the loco shed for engines and general supply. Water for drinking purposes was carried in rail tanks from Kemble in Gloucestershire until 1902.

The opening of the stores, and the operation of the mill, secured employment for around thirty local men, quite a boost to the community. Most of the work was of an unskilled nature giving the youth of the district an alternative to farming; once again the farmers were competing for labour.

There was an ironic turn of events to this; when fodder was required for the mill it was the local farmers who were in the most favourable position to be the suppliers, if they had the staff to do so. Somehow, in spite of this, they were able to manage, as it is well known locally that some of the farmers were better off as a result of the provender mill.

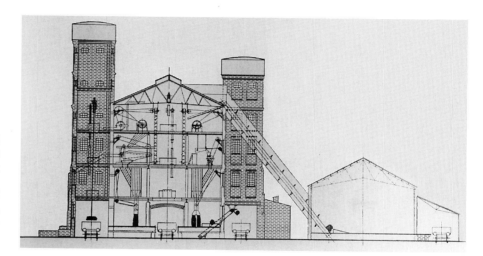

Right: The provender store in line drawing from the same aspect as the previous picture. *Author's collection*

Below: A picture taken from the rear of the transfer shed in the early 1900s. The reservoir water is low prior to the raising of the dam.

A short wheelbase 'Simplex' petrol-mechanical loco, used to shunt wagons on the provender sidings after the horses were withdrawn. The one at Didcot was GWR departmental loco No.26, built by Motor Rail Ltd of Bedford, their No.4178 of 1927. It came to the provender stores from new and eventually went to Swindon Works for scrap in 1960.

British Rail

The amount of foodstuffs needed was far in excess of their ability to supply. Tenders were put out and supplies obtained from many parts of the country. The fodder and feed brought in was put under the most severe scrutiny. It was claimed that each bale of hay was individually examined and if any should not meet the stringent requirements it was returned to the supplier at his own cost, thus setting the highest of standards.

Almost all consignments arriving had been loaded at a railway station under a free voucher scheme, the farmer only having to pay for any rejects which were returned. All transactions were dealt with in the goods shed adjoining the transfer shed. The incoming wagons were usually detached in batches from trains calling at Didcot to detach in general, and were left in the west end sidings to wait for the pilot engine to place them in position.

Often we went as far as the entrance to position the full wagons at the platform. When the wagons had been emptied, depending on the type of wagon, or whether it was needed, it would be taken right through the building and out the other end by the use of a cart horse, with ropes and capstans, to be placed either at another platform for loading or shunted into a siding for dispatch.

The wagons for carrying hay and straw were built either with high sides (seven planks as opposed to the standard five), or were modified standard wagons with a double rail round the top to give extra capacity for this light but bulky load. All these wagons were sheeted to protect the contents from the weather. Corn, oats and maize usually arrived in sacks in box vans.

In 1927 the working horses were withdrawn and a small petrol engine was introduced. The little engine was specially designed to negotiate the very tight curves within the sidings. To accomplish this the wheelbase was only a fraction more than its track was wide. Although the engine was very low in horse power, it had a huge reduction gear which made it quite a powerful machine for its size, as such, it was able to move several wagons together, but only slowly, not much faster than the horse.

The provision of stores for the mill was not always as regular as the company would have liked. There were years when crops were of a poor standard, and at times stocks fell low, giving rise to concern regarding continuity of supplies. The storage space did not allow for contingency stores, and it was inconceivable that during these difficult periods supplies should go direct to the horses without treatment and examination.

To ease this situation, a new building was constructed in 1900 at the rear of the main building, for the purpose of maintaining a larger stock of hay and straw. This released space inside the main building for extra storage of cereal crops; the new building was appropriately called the hay barn. The structure was of brick in the manner of the main building with wood and slated roof and a skylight along its entire length. The total length was 163ft with a width of 48ft, totalling 7,824 sq ft in area, and with a height of 27ft was capable of holding a very large

reserve. A rail line ran along the entire length of the building with an unloading platform. From inside the barn the truss of hay was lifted by an angled elevator to the top of the building, where it received its first treatment.

A local newspaper reporter wrote an article in 1937 on the merits of the stores:

A hay diet for horses; this is nothing new, and for 52 years now the Great Western Railway Provender Stores at Didcot have supplied the mixtures of hay and corn that the hard working horses all over the railway system have needed for their meals.

In fact, every day food is being made at Didcot, that is, so to speak, generating many thousand horse power.

There are between 1,700 to 1,800 horses at work on goods and parcels delivery for the GWR in various parts of England and Wales today, and dinner for all these comes from this tall Berkshire factory, that stands with its high towers and elevator by the main line at Didcot.

Generally speaking, the factory receives cereal crops and hay, and after preparing and mixing them to the prescribed standard, sends it out for the horses' meal. Sleeping straw is also received and sent out as required.

During the early months of 1941 I was working on the shunting pilot with my mate, Bert East, placing wagons in one of the unloading bays. Although I had been at Didcot for several months I was still curious to know just what went on in the building. I questioned Bert for information, His reply was:

'I don't really know, go inside and take a look. There's nothing much to do, I can manage for a while.'

I tentatively looked inside, it was just as stark as the outside, all I could see was the loading platforms. As I stood there, a man who appeared to be an official enquired whether I was interested in looking round. Without any further thought for my mate left on the engine, I accepted his offer. He took me up the spiral staircase to the third floor, explaining that the top floor only received meal. Hay went up the sloping outside elevator which I did not witness, but inside a vertical elevator was gently running with scoops attached carrying loose corn; it rattled and clattered as it tipped its contents into large bins. From here the corn was taken through a series of processes including drying and having the dust taken off before being loaded into sacks. Short elevators and continuously moving belts added to the general noise, in some cases loose grain shook its way along one belt to drop on to another one going at right angles. Husks were separated and took another route to be disposed of.

I was interested mainly in the seemingly complicated machinery which was duplicated on both sides of the factory with so many conveyor belts, some of which were acting as grading machines.

Back down to the second floor and we came to the mixing machines; this was really the crux of the matter, the various grades of corn and chaff were being mixed to dispatch to different areas. Each horse had its own diet according to the type of work it was doing and the area in which it was working.

Also on this floor there was a series of hot water pipes to form drying racks for the sacks. Everything in the way of meal was taken away by sack, it was important that the sacks were properly dried before filling. The drying area had a stuffy damp atmosphere and elsewhere in the building there was a countryfied air, sparrows lived and nested in the building, particularly on the top floor, I was told.

It was very important to keep a watch on the temperature of the corn and hay; there was always the possibility of spontaneous combustion, to guard against this a sprinkler system was installed in 1932.

Bert wasn't too pleased when I eventually returned, he asked sharply:

'Where have you been all this time? I've been waiting for you to go back across to the yard.'

The provender store not only took care of the horses' meals as a matter of daily routine, but also took care of their welfare, in a field adjoining the west curve. When a horse needed a rest or recuperation it was brought here to wander about the field and eat fresh grass. Of the thousands of horses employed, they were so well taken care of, that no more than eight to ten could be seen at any time.

The machinery in use on my visit was driven by electric motors; it had not always been like that. When the mill was first built it was driven by steam power, shafts ran along the top of the walls driven by belts from the engine below in the boiler house. The rotating shafts had pulleys along their length positioned to drive a machine by secondary belts. With a number of machines already clattering, the din must have been almost insufferable with the added slapping and smacking of the belts; in my youth I worked in a factory with such antiquated machinery and I found it quite distressing. These belts were unprotected and should they break there was the distinct possibility of serious injury to the operator.

On 8 August 1900 steam power was substituted by electric power, the current being generated in the power house of the mill.

An order from Swindon Stores Department was headed:

Provision of Plant including a spare engine and electrical generator for obtaining a water supply; The appliance will be sufficient to supply water to the parishes of Didcot and Hagbourne, for which they are willing to pay at the rate of 6d per 1,000 gallons. Cost £5,500.

December 1900.

The mill functioned well for many years but the life span of the machinery was fast coming to an end. In 1925 the Stores Committee held a meeting to consider replacing the old machines, many of which were still being driven by the communal belts. The decision was taken to replace all the machinery drive with individual electric motors.

Some of the workmen were a little apprehensive about having to work with the electric motors so near to them, these were early days and the men needed convincing that there was no danger.

The minutes of the Stores Committee meeting held on 26 March 1926 read:

Installation of the new machinery at Didcot provender stores. The contract was duly placed with Messrs Porteus & Co., and the installation of new machinery has been completed.

The new machinery has been running since September 1925 and it is now possible to report on the economies which have ensued.

It has been possible to reduce the staff by eight men, representing an annual saving of £1,176. The electrical current for operating the machinery has been reduced from 7,000 units to 5,000 units a month and it is anticipated that the maintenance of the new plant, owing to its improved construction, will represent an additional economy which will be ascertainable in twelve months time.

The quality of the provender produced from the new plant is superior to that of the old, it being cleared of the dust and being more uniformly mixed, sufficient extraction resulting in more healthy conditions for the men engaged.

It is considered that this machinery will have a beneficial effect on the life and stability of the building owing to the entire removal of heavy vibration which was inseparable from the use of the old plant. The new plant occupies less space than the old which can now be used as extra storage space for hay which is valuable.

As can be gathered, the mill was not only a source of employment but by the use of its water pump the village was now having the luxury of running water. Until this time the only supply was from the unreliable wells.

In 1902 the newly formed Rural District Council had a water tower built at Manor Farm to ensure a constant supply to the village. It was at this time when the provender pumps first drew water from the well at Appleford, the new pumps were quite adequate for this extra work, being described as 'two three-throw ram pumps driven by electric motors at 10hp with reduction gear by current generated by the provender mill.'

There were several ancillary buildings; a covered one for the road vehicle, but no mention of a stable for the horse; a rail weighbridge house; firewood store; boiler house; coal bin; foreman's office; salt house; mess room; and later a petrol store when the horse was finally retired in favour of the petrol engine.

The estimated cost of the original building together with the outbuildings was £19,507.

The provender mill horse was displaced by the more favourable motor lorry, and therefore it follows that the rest of the railway system would follow this principle. As

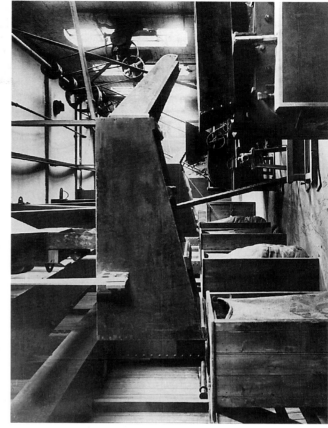

Top left: An insight into the provender stores generator room, also showing the water pumping machinery. **Top right:** The hay barn with a bale of hay starting its journey to the top of the mill. The elevator was driven by electric motor. **Bottom left:** The provender corn store with bins to the left and sacks to the right. **Bottom right:** The system of chutes and troughs delivering the corn to the bagging area.

W Pereira

a consequence the number of horses employed by the railway dropped dramatically, but the mill was needed to carry on with a much smaller staff for a considerable time. In 1930 the mill ceased generating electricity, a supply was obtained from the Southern Electricity Board at 11,000 volts, transformed to 400 volts by transformers situated within the power house.

When all the horses were eventually withdrawn the mill was closed in 1953. For a short time it was let to the Pressed Steel Company of Oxford and finally demolished in April of 1967, changing the local landscape considerably.

The reservoir which had served such good purpose for so many years was partially filled in with rubble from the demolished buildings. Later the filling in was completed and the ground made level to be used as a car park.

It was hoped, that by making this a free car park, customers would be attracted from the surrounding area to Didcot station, which was then renamed Didcot Parkway.

The site of the provender stores today. Gone are the mill, the reservoir and the West End signal box. The motor car has taken over the area for parking, giving the name Didcot Parkway to the station. *Author's collection*

80

CHAPTER NINE

Development

The opening of the station gave the first opportunity for regular employment, that is to say, except for farming. To these humble people this was indeed a great step forward, and when the provender mill opened many more found work. Prospects certainly looked much better for them, but they were still living in a little backwater.

The construction labourers had left, in their place came the men who were to work the railway. Accommodation was at a premium, houses were small and in most cases overcrowded. Until now there had been no need for additional houses, except in the minds of local speculators, one of which, a local business man, made the first move. He had a small row of terrace houses built at the eastern end of the village in the mid 1880s, solely for letting to railwaymen. A few years later two more short rows of cottages were built some way to the east of the station, where the line crossed the turnpike road, at a point called Hagbourne Marsh. The cottages subsequently became known as the Marsh Cottages and stand to this day. Again the rents were high which effectively reserved them for the better paid railwaymen.

The land under cultivation in the area was not readily available for building on, that is, not until a farmer named Thomas Higgs of East Hagbourne put up a large plot for sale in 1886. The whole plot of 9 acres was sold to George Dixon for £6,130. The site covered an area mainly to the west of Hagbourne Road and bounded by the Wallingford Road on its northern side. It is uncertain what the original object of the purchase was, but it is known that very little time elapsed before George Dixon had divided the land into neat little plots in straight rows. Soon the plots were to be sold off in small batches. The first of these sales was for eight plots together, fronting on to Wallingford Road. Within a year some of the houses were being occupied, again with a predominance of railwaymen, and within seven years of the original purchase there were more than seventy houses built. Various speculators built these houses mainly for renting, there was no conformity, except that they were all built in straight lines. These houses still stand today and reflect the mood and ideas of the many builders, which add to the charm of this unique development.

Mr Dixon, by laying out the plots as he did in straight lines, and making a pattern of roads, did, in effect, set a standard of planning.

The size of the area of land bought by Mr Dixon and the direction in which it was being used indicated that a community was developing there, which indeed it did. This created the need for a church of some denomination and as a result a Methodist church was built. Later the Wesleyans also built their church and for a time the two functioned until there was a merger of the two churches.

The building of new houses in this area was almost completed by the turn of the century with Mr Dixon holding the larger share of the ownership, his being in excess of twenty plots with several small contractors and a few private builders in the minority, with none having more than six plots.

A new community of this size could not exist without trades people and retail shops. To fulfil this need some of the local people became entrepreneurs, opening shops such as grocery, butcher, hardware, shoe repairers and later a cycle shop.

The GWR acquired a house in Monkton Street in 1879 specially for a railway servant. The first occupant was Mr Steel, a locomotive foreman who was reported as always wearing a top hat; much the same as the station master. Among other things, a public house was built and named *The Sprat*, which was well patronised by the railwaymen now living there.

To most people the new development became known as New Town, even to the residents of Old Didcot who still treated it as a separate community, with very little direct contact.

The railway had in effect created this division by building Station Hill. This new and better road to connect with the turnpike road – now known as Wallingford Road – led directly towards the area now developed. Had they chosen to connect with a better road towards the village, who knows what the outcome would have been?

The new town lay to the east of Station Hill and all to the west was regarded as Didcot. There was not only a distance between them but also a social barrier, each keeping to its own. No doubt the new shops in the new town drew some custom from the old village, but probably only those in railway employ, who would find themselves more readily accepted and with more money to spend.

The local recognition of New Town is noted in the

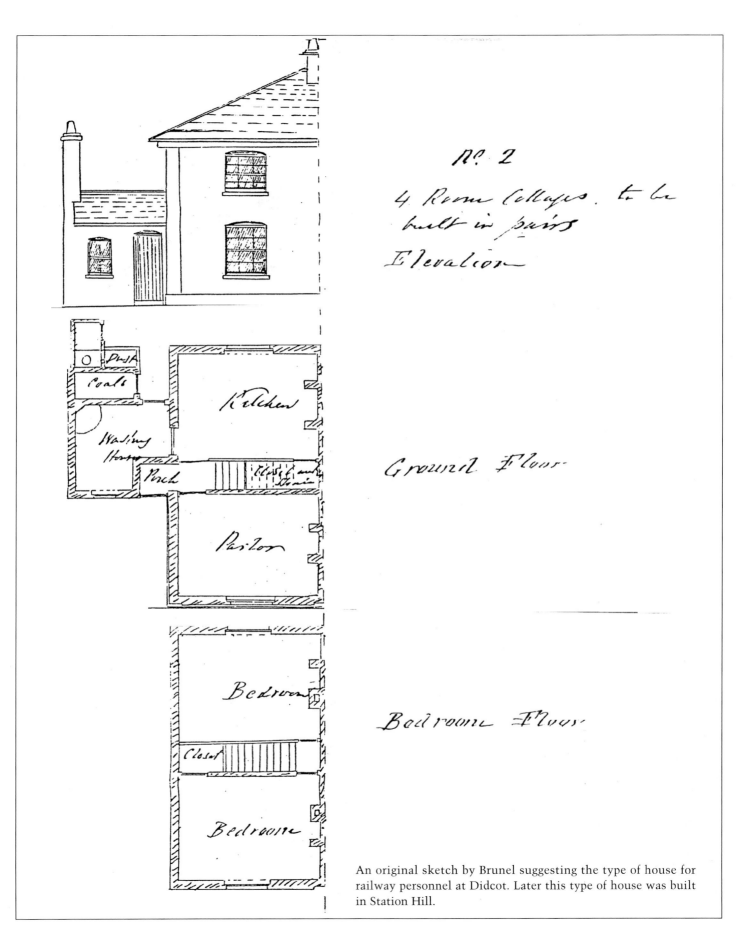

N.º 2
4 Room Cottages. to be
built in pairs
Elevation

Ground Floor

Bedroom Floor

An original sketch by Brunel suggesting the type of house for railway personnel at Didcot. Later this type of house was built in Station Hill.

heading of a notice of auction of some plots of land in 1904:

Auction of land in Hagbourne Road and Church Road. New Town. 29 September 1904. At this auction George Davies Junior, coal merchant, for his wife Martha, bought property in Hagbourne Road (three plots for building) at the price of £60; £5 deposit to secure.

In 1905 the GWR bought a row of six small cottages which were built by Mr Wheeler of Wantage to accommodate other railwaymen.

Although Brunel had suggested houses to be built in Station Hill as far back as 1846 when the road was made, there was a gap of fifty years before the plan was resurrected. In 1897 work was commenced on the building of twenty cottages for railway staff, and were designated to the various departments in 1899 as follows:

Erection of houses for the use of staff –

Stores department	4 houses of D standard
Loco and Carriage	1 house of B standard
" "	4 houses of C standard
" "	4 houses of D standard

In addition later; one for permanent way inspector and six for PW men; four cottages for telegraph department, and in 1906 two standard D type for the linesmen deputed to look after the electrical installation; cost £508.

These cottages were considered to be extraordinary, originally designed by Brunel in 1846, they were supplied with gas from the company's own gas works at the loco shed where it was first made in 1862. At that time the station, shed, and yards benefited from this new source of lighting. In later years when carriages were gas lit they each had a reservoir maintained from this same source. When the Station Hill buildings were completed a few gas lamps were installed in the road; the first street lighting in Didcot.

At the same time the water supply which was provided by the provender mill was laid to all the houses.

Another first for the houses was when two of them were fitted with baths and hot and cold water on tap. These houses, although on the western side of the road, were always thought of as being in Northbourne, but many saw them as being in Hagbourne. This compounded the disagreement by adding a fourth dimension. There was now a reference to Didcot, Old Didcot, New Town and Northbourne. Eventually the name was settled as Northbourne for this area.

In a later entry in *Cassey's Directory*, before the advent of Northbourne, there is shown an improvement in the recognition of Didcot; obviously due to the coming of the railway:

It is a respectable village and parish, five miles from Abingdon, fifty three miles from London by the Great Western Railway, and ten miles from Oxford, in the hundred of Moreton, union of Wallingford, and diocese of Oxford.

This is a station and junction of the Oxford Birmingham line. The Church of All Saints is a handsome edifice, with a wood shingle spire. The living is a rectory, annual value £397, with residence, in the patronage of the Principal and Fellows of Brasenose College, Oxford; the Revd John Ashworth, MA, is incumbent.

There is a corn exchange and a market held on a Tuesday. Here is a Sunday school and a national school. The population in 1861 was 349; the area is 1,097 acres of good arable land. Col. Loyd-Lindsey (Lord of the Manor) and Jacob Appleford, Esq, are the landowners. John Andrews is the post master and letters arrive through Wallingford at 10am and are dispatched at 5pm.

A gathering of the men employed in construction of the houses in Station Hill c1900, many displaying the tools of their trade.

Author's collection

There was no one responsible for development until 1894 when the Wallingford District Council was formed, whose priorities were soon recognised as being far more serious than town planning; much more pressing needs were on the agenda. Old Didcot was in a terrible run down condition.

In an assessment of the problems, Mr A. Bullen wrote an article headed 'Wallingford Rural District Council'.

The only urban development was at Newtown or Northbourne, as it became known. The public health situation was primitive and it took well over twenty years to clear this up. The sanitation, drainage and water supply had not changed for hundreds of years, being primitive in the extreme.

Working class houses were appalling, in most cases sub-standard; houses were in most cases damp, badly constructed and in most cases overcrowded. It took many years to overcome this situation.

Cholera had been eliminated from the district by 1890. (Many other parts of the country had succeeded some forty or fifty years before this).

The first system of main drainage in the district was installed for Didcot and North Hagbourne between 1897 and 1903. A mains water supply was also installed at the same time for these two parishes.

The flurry of activity which had encompassed both the railway and the local community around the turn of the century was now subsiding. Northbourne was now almost completed, only the odd house being built here and there. Wantage Road had a plot occupied occasionally but elsewhere progress was rather static.

The railway had also completed their house building programme, except for the two houses for the electricians responsible for the maintenance of the electrical North Junction box.

The expansion of the railway was almost at a standstill, the extra lines needed, together with the new junctions and associated signal boxes were now capable of carrying the volume of traffic of the day.

There was now a lull in development for about ten years, until the start of the Great War. The army was aware that their arsenal at Woolwich in London was in a vulnerable position, situated as it was in the Thames estuary, and in a position where it was feared that attacks could be made upon it, either from the air by the German Zeppelins, or even from the water. With this in mind they looked for a safer site, somewhere inland, more central and with good communications. Taking a similar view to that of the railway when the company built the provender mill, they also chose Didcot as their site, taking advantage of the rail network with distribution to all points.

Towards the end of 1914 the War Office acquired a large area of land on the northern side of the main line and to the west of Foxhall junction, proceeding right away to build their new ordnance depot. Many huge sheds were to be erected in a series of straight lines, with rows of similar lines across. Subsequently the sheds were numbered A1 to A5 across the first row followed by B1 to B5 and so on to D row. At this

point a considerable gap was left and later other rows were added, numbered E, F, and so on. Much later even more sheds were added, sprawling the depot a long way towards Appleford.

Each shed was 400ft long by 64ft wide which included the platform for loading from the railway side and the canopy to cover the platform.

Pairs of these sheds faced each other in rows with three railway lines running between them, the middle line being for through movements, while the lines to each side were platform lines with a set of points each end for the purpose of shunting. These sets of lines between the sheds were referred to as gulleys, each had its own pilot engine to carry out the shunting, all the engines supplied from Didcot loco.

With the sheds arranged as they were, a wide gap was left between them which was used as an internal road system, these roads crossed the railway lines at each end of the sheds on a level crossing, often a cause for concern during shunting movements. The gulleys were numbered and with later expansion reached number five, from which a line extended right through to the Royal Flying Corps depot at Milton.

Railway connections were established at Foxhall with an outlet to the up main line, with a further junction to the west curve leading to the north. Road access was via the Foxhall bridge with another bridge built to cross the line.

The land acquired for laying the west curve had been purchased from Col.R.J. Lindsay in August of 1884. Adjoining land used to lay the main line had previously been purchased from Brasenose College, Oxford in 1883. This left the depot site partly in the hands of Brasenose College and part to Lord Appleford.

The first signal box opened at Foxhall in 1874 had insufficient frame capacity to operate the new points and signals. It was closed in 1915 when it was superseded by a new box.

The new ordnance depot received considerable publicity. One article written in December 1915 gives its observations:

The urgencies of the war and the need for greater facilities for the manufacture of war materials, have decided the War Office Officials to supplement the Woolwich Arsenal with an inland auxiliary, and Didcot has been selected for the site. No less than 280 acres of land has been purchased.

Didcot is very favourably situated for an arsenal. There is the Great Western Railway station with direct communications with the north, south, east and west, and it is said that communications will be established with the Thames by cutting a canal from Appleford, starting 200 or 300 yards on the upstream side of the railway bridge. The making of this would be both easy and inexpensive.

Very intensive operations will be carried on, giving employment to a great number of people. This will entirely alter the whole character of the neighbourhood. Didcot, which has for so long been in a semi-dormant state will soon be as busy as any part of Berkshire.

Although the arsenal will stand in no less than five parishes, the largest portion by far will be in Didcot.

The recent stagnation in growth was inevitable, little or no industry had been generated by the coming of the railway. It is true that the influx of railwaymen and the development of Northbourne with its new tradesmen had done a little for the local economy. It is also true that most of these workers would by now have grown-up families looking for work and the new depot probably relieved this situation as much as it created needs.

At the time the depot was being constructed the council was requested to supply 300 new houses for the incoming workers from London and that when the depot was completed another 300 houses would be needed.

The council was also in difficulties with its water supply. By the middle of June 1916 the army was expected to be requiring an estimated 45,000 gallons of water a week, in the event it was found to be using 5,000 gallons in excess of that. The population of Didcot and Northbourne were seen to suffer most of the hardship by being deprived of water during the daylight hours. The army, aware of the situation, developed an additional supply, but still required the council to provide more. The council, which was obliged to the railway for its supplies, passed on the request. The GWR, which was now supplying water from its well at Appleford, wrote in August 1916 'We are now unable to increase supplies.' As a result Didcot and Hagbourne suffered water shortages until 1928; it was about this time when the council built its own waterworks.

This rather dreary period of stagnation ceased when the Second World War started in 1939. The difficulties associated with the first war were repeated once again. The logistics, being more intense this time, put an even greater strain on the ordnance depot; the railway, too, became much more involved.

The complacency which had shrouded Didcot over the last two decades turned more to anxiety than fear. Realising that in the First World War the ordnance depot was quite safe from the enemy, they had no fears, but times had changed, and enemy planes could quite easily penetrate this far inland. This army depot which had for so long been a mainstay of employment, now became a threat. After all, it was originally built as an arsenal for the production and storage of munitions, and with the Royal Air Force depot adjoining the Milton end, it was considered by most to be a prime target for enemy bombers.

The forebodings which had surrounded the depot manifested themselves one night an hour or so before midnight some six weeks after the war started. The initial fears had lessened, until the night the air raid warning sounded. Those of us at work in the depot waited and wondered. The military took to the shelters, leaving us to our fate, but not before giving us strict instructions not to show any lights and to keep the fire-hole doors closed. There was an eerie silence as we scanned the sky and strained our ears; after about two hours the all-clear sounded, but not a sight nor sound did we encounter.

It ultimately transpired as the years passed that the depot was not of sufficient importance to the enemy to warrant attacks. In fact, the only bomb which fell in the neighbourhood was a stick of about five small bombs which straddled the railway line near to the Milton RAF depot, doing no damage. It seems that a lone marauder flying low jettisoned its bombs and ran for home just as dawn was breaking.

The view from the lineside to the west of Foxhall junction showing several of the camouflaged sheds within the ordnance depot.
British Rail

Foxhall junction in June 1933 looking west. The new signal box, brought into use in October 1931, is prominent in the centre of the picture. A Dean 0-6-0 is on the west curve facing towards Oxford, with part of the ordnance depot in the background. The wagons are standing on the local goods line, and being from the SR, LMS and NE, emphasise that traffic at Didcot came from all directions.

Mowat collection

Didcot Station

A GWR country bus leaving Didcot station in the early 1920s.

In the period between the two wars during which the railways had the monopoly on transport, the motor car was only making small inroads into the business. Transport from the station was normally by small horse-drawn carriages, in most cases the type known as a 'Fly'. These vehicles plied from most station forecourts.

The horse-drawn vehicle met the same fate as its commercial counterpart, displaced by the motor car and buses.

The GWR, perhaps unwittingly, opened up a local bus service in competition to its own railway service. It started a service in the Didcot area with the buses based at Wantage, radiating from there at first to Swindon in November 1924, followed by a service to Didcot in December 1925, with other services to Challow and East Hanney in 1928. There was also a short-lived service coming into Didcot from Newbury on Tuesdays and Thursdays during the summer of 1928 for the market. The GWR also branched out to run tours from Wantage in the summers of 1927/28 to the downs, visiting White Horse Hill and Waylands Smithy, a local beauty spot.

Ultimately other new bus companies sprang up in competition with the railway, which in turn, felt obliged to buy large interests in these companies to protect its own revenue.

Between the wars the general depression affected the railways which were losing traffic for the first time, and the hitherto sinecure position of the workforce was now being threatened; the management asked them to take a three per cent reduction in pay.

Eventually, when the difficulties were resolved, the Great Western, still in financial trouble, attempted to bolster its economy by introducing a system of coal saving with a coal bonus scheme for footplatemen.

There are few people around today who are able to recall how the system worked. Some of the older drivers with whom I worked sometimes talked of the problems surrounding this ill-founded scheme. When an engine was coaled the full tubs represented a given amount in weight, usually ten hundredweight. As always, the amount was recorded to each engine and kept on record. At this period in time each driver had his own engine, unless his was in for servicing, and he took a spare. This way every driver could be related to the amount of coal used.

A set amount of coal was assessed for each type of engine and the driver paid a bonus for whatever he saved below that amount. To make this worthwhile the driver would have to work his engine as lightly as possible, but worse still, he watched every knob of coal the fireman put on the fire, controlling his every move. The drivers even shut off steam early in an effort to conserve fuel, regardless of time keeping.

I worked with men who had suffered at the hands of the bonus drivers, some of whom had been afflicted by the idea and were almost as bad as their mentors, persistently interfering with the fireman. It made for tedious working, but obviously not anywhere near as unbearable as the real thing, the two men were often at loggerheads with each other.

Many tales were told of drivers stealing from another engine, and even going to work on a Sunday morning, ostensibly to clean and oil their engine, but with the coal bonus in mind.

One can conjure up a picture of several drivers all scheming to raid each others' engines but at the same time watching their own.

The fireman was always the one to suffer the most and had the misery of it all, yet he didn't partake of any of the benefits. It was a very unfair scheme and all were glad when it came to an end.

Didcot locomotive allocation at 1 January 1948:

4-6-0:	5903, 5935, 6923, 6952
4-4-0:	3376, 3396, 3408, 3419, 3448, 9006, 9015, 9083
2-6-0:	4318, 4326, 5330, 5380, 5381, 5397, 6329, 6359, 6379
2-4-0:	1334
0-6-0:	2202, 2221, 2226, 2240, 2252, 2289, 2532, 3210, 3211, 3212
2-8-2T:	7204, 7214, 7228, 7252
0-6-0PT:	907, 1861, 3622, 3709, 3721, 4601, 5710, 5735, 5744, 5752, 7710
2-8-0 WD:	70843 (90327), 79303 (90725)
Service loco:	26
0-6-0:	2222 Outstabled at Newbury
0-4-2T:	Outstabled at Wallingford (Provided from Reading)

CHAPTER TEN

Decline and Modernisation

The long years of war also took their toll of the physical aspects of the railway. Everything concerned had fallen into a dilapidated condition. The track, stock and, in particular, the locomotives were all in a seriously run down condition. Swindon Works had been pre-occupied with the war effort, engines were only given as much attention as was necessary to keep them in service. Considering the state they were allowed to get in they did remarkably well, the problems with steaming stemmed mainly from the difficulties within the loco sheds, so many engines passing through their hands daily made it quite impossible to keep them up to standard.

Climbing aboard one of these unkempt engines, whether to prepare it or perhaps to relieve on the road, set one back a little. The old Great Western livery was suspended and they were all painted black just to keep them tidy looking. There were no cleaners in the sheds which allowed the engines to become exceeding drab.

Passenger stock also became very untidy, the tender care with which up to twenty coats of paint and varnish was applied had to be reduced, likewise the interior could not have the attention it deserved. Freight wagons, which were already old fashioned, were almost on their last legs, most only capable of the restricted work they had been doing.

With the end of the war there was a comparatively rapid return to the standards of the GWR, it didn't show for a little time until the first locos came out of Swindon refurbished and resplendent in the Great Western livery of Brunswick green with the orange and black lining, and the brasswork shining once more.

Coaching stock also took on a new shine and in an attempt to create a new image experiments were carried out using various colours. None matched those which had been imprinted on our minds for so long; chocolate and cream.

Soon the famous name of the Great Western Railway was to be lost for ever, only to be preserved in the memory of those who had lived with it, and for it.

On 1 January 1948 the four main line companies were nationalised to be known as The Railway Commission. This did nothing to boost the pride of the railwaymen, the men of each company all felt that their identity was lost. It was a long time before the loco men of the GWR came

to terms with the change, but they never forgot their allegiance.

Nationalisation was soon followed by rationalisation which meant savage cuts in an attempt to make the railways pay for themselves. The appointment of Dr Beeching on 31 December 1962 to oversee the cuts was considered by all railwaymen to be a disastrous move. The main aim in the first instance was to eliminate all unprofitable branch lines. This may have seemed practicable at the time, except that most branch lines were feeders for the main lines; it was once said, 'It's like cutting your arms off to make your body better.' Didcot's victim was, of course, the Newbury & Southampton line, but before this happened there was a final fling. The passenger numbers on the line had never been strong, but the line was still a very useful route, as recent events had proved.

In 1957/58 the Commission decided it was time to rekindle the interest of the public. To this end the famous locomotive *City of Truro* was taken out of York Railway Museum and overhauled at Swindon Works. From there it was sent to Didcot and booked regularly on the 7.38am passenger train to Southampton. Of all the branches on the Great Western this particular line most suited this loco. Unfortunately, although there was ample enthusiasm for the loco, it failed in its main object of drawing in more revenue. Passenger traffic continued to fall off resulting in the withdrawal of the loco from this service and for a while it ran two trains a day to Paddington until being returned to a museum.

The branch line service was reduced and for a while diesel multiple units were employed as a cost cutting exercise. On 7 March 1960 the southern section from Newbury to Shawford junction was closed to passenger traffic, but freight trains were still using the route; the end was in sight.

Local goods traffic on this section was ordered to be taken either to the Newbury or Winchester main line stations. Heavy freight trains were still running at the rate of twelve trains a day for a period, often hauled by the newly designed standard class 9F 2-10-0. By this time Southern Region men had taken over much of the train work and had become a common sight working into Didcot.

On 10 September 1962 all passenger services ceased on

Due to the coal shortage in 1946 the government encouraged the railways to convert engines to oil burning. The GWR planned conversion of 63 28xx, 84 49xx and 25 'Castles'. Didcot was included in the list of depots to have oil plants installed. This picture shows the newly laid additional line adjoining the turntable road with the extensive fuelling apron and the standard arrangement of three 12,000 gallon oil tanks, (144 tons total). The brick-built pumping house is seen beyond the end of the storage tanks. A stores van stands on the fuelling road while a 'Busby' fitted 0-6-0PT stands by the shed and a 43xx Mogul slowly steams away from the coal stage towards the turntable. The fuel point was never used to its full advantage due to the unsuccessful conversion to oil.

British Rail

No.3440 *City of Truro* arriving at Didcot east bay with a return train from Southampton during its visit from York Museum.
Lens of Sutton

A passenger's view of *City of Truro* as it takes the curve from Didcot east bay onto the branch line.
R M Casserley

Mogul No.9307 with extended buffer beam and square cab stands alongside the lifting shop. *Author's collection*

0-6-0PT No.1502 with Walschaerts valve gear but not fitted with superheater stands by the side of the lifting shop, in about 1958. Behind is an earlier generation of shunting loco, 0-6-0PT No.5742. *R S Carpenter*

Didcot shed c1960 with steam and diesel mixed. A diesel shunter and a 'Hymek' stand in number six road.   *E Wilmshurst*

4-4-0 ex Southern Railway 3P No.30285 off a Southampton passenger service. Note the inevitable tea can at the ready. A Collett 22xx class 0-6-0 heads a petrol tank train from the branch to the avoiding line – the two barrier wagons between the loco and the train were a requirement in the days of steam.   *R C Riley*

A 'Castle' class heading the *Capitals United Express* on the down main.   *Author's collection*

Didcot based No.6937 *Conyngham Hall* stands on the up relief line with an express parcels train in December 1963.
Merchant Navy Locomotive Preservation Society

the northern section Didcot to Newbury. Although the section had been earmarked for complete closure in June of 1964 it did in fact stay open until the final closure of the whole line on 9 August of that year. The final demise came when the track was lifted in 1967.

The first major attempt at modernisation was getting designs for a series of twelve standard locomotives with the aim of eliminating the multitude of old fashioned and various types of engines. In effect the principle was to wipe out all the previous railway's outdated types and replace them with locos which would be compatible to all regions. To achieve this, hundreds of new locos would have to be built. However, standardisation of locos did not reach fruition, the numbers were slow to come off the production lines and the whole concept was overtaken by dieselisation. It was not therefore surprising when in March 1956 the Western Region took delivery of its first main line diesel hydraulic locos, numbered D600. These were followed a year later by the D800 class, of which there were seventy-five built, and quickly on their heels came the smaller D7000 class, also the D6300, a single engined version of the D800 with the MAN engine and the Voith transmission.

Marvellous tales were told of the supremacy of the new diesels working the West of England passenger trains. The men were enthusiastically telling tales of how the diesels could clip the running times by amounts unheard of, and with the fireman sitting in a comfortable seat, only needing to tend the train steam heating boiler occasionally.

Unfortunately, mere mortals like myself, who were interested in the machines, were not allowed to even look in the cab, let alone get on board. It was understandable because so many maintenance staff needed to monitor the performance and to learn more about what they were now expected to maintain. An inspector accompanied these locos in the first instance and then there were tutor drivers with men to train; too many people with needs, like bees round a honey pot, to allow anyone like me to get a look in.

The majority of the Western Region local passenger services were by now being worked by diesel multiple units, practically all the 61xx 2-6-2 Prairie tank engines were eliminated from passenger work.

In the transitional period Didcot loco accommodated diesel locos with a fuelling point adjacent to the line going down to the turntable. No main line diesels were allocated to Didcot.

'Modified Hall' class No.7929, with name and number plates already removed, is nearing withdrawal, but taking on coal at Didcot in 1965.
J R Fairman

Engines which appear to be in good condition stand at the rear of Didcot shed. Judging by their empty tenders they have been withdrawn from service.
J R Fairman

38xx class 2-8-0 with number and shed plates removed at the rear of the shed in February 1965 having been withdrawn.
J R Fairman

At the same time as the steam engines were being laid up more and more of these were dumped in what became known as the grave yard at the rear of the shed. Here they were allowed to rust away, their tenders emptied of coal and looking all forlorn, slowly being cannibalised for spare parts to keep others in service.

Didcot was among the first casualties of dieselisation when the steam shed was closed 14 June 1965. Until the diesel programme got under way there were as many as seventeen main line locos allocated to the shed. All went to scrap eventually, perhaps an odd one may have been rescued from the cutters torch and preserved for posterity.

The closure of the shed also made the drivers and firemen homeless, they were accommodated in a new building in the goods yard together with the guards and inspectors. Their numbers had been drastically reduced, some took redundancy and early retirement, quite happy to leave rather than change the habits of a lifetime on steam working.

The closure of the ordnance depot in the previous year had already reduced the ranks of the train crews and this new loss quite reversed the status of railwaymen at Didcot. From the time the railway was built until now railwaymen were in a sinecure position, a job for life. Now only a small body of men was left for the purpose of train relief work; a far cry from the days of the war when they were numbered in the hundreds.

The Central Electricity Generating Board built a new power station on the site of the previous ordnance depot. This redressed the situation a little by providing employment for a number of local men, including some of the railwaymen who were made redundant.

Trains arrived into the finished power station bringing in stocks some months before electricity production began. Didcot men were not favoured with any of the incoming workings, all the trains arriving were manned by men from other depots, those in the colliery areas.

The closure of the provender mill earlier had no adverse effect upon the locomen, footplatemen had never been involved even at the height of its working.

As a further result of nationalisation and the cancellation of all stopping passenger trains to Swindon on 7 December 1964 all the stations on the route were subsequently closed. The original station at Steventon, once a focal point of the GWR, already having been relegated from its position of importance, now fell to the same fate, soon to be demolished and just a memory.

The closure of these stations together with the closure of the Newbury line made both the east and west bays unnecessary and they too were taken out of use, leaving the remainder of the platforms to be renumbered.

Each of these wayside stations had its goods yard and goods shed for dealing with parcels and packages for local delivery. With the stations and their associated goods

Inside the transfer shed looking east towards the station. The original broad gauge line is on the right. One of the replacement cranes is in the foreground amongst the debris of disuse.

W Pereira

97

departments gone the stopping goods trains which served them also went. The knock-on effect quickly ran through the system culminating in the closure of the Didcot goods shed. Once an integral part of Brunel's strategy for the development of Didcot, it had in the past been demoted from a transfer shed to being a goods shed, now it was closed altogether. To the men, its original name of the transfer shed was held to the end. It stood in an unused and slowly dilapidating state until it was finally removed for preservation.

The general loss of freight traffic on the region caused many closures, one of which was the wartime marshalling yard at Moreton cutting, the work there had slowly contracted and it was finally closed in 1964 with the loss of several more jobs. Soon the associated goods loops and sidings were recovered, leaving the land to nature.

Many reductions were made in the interest of economy, some were forced upon the Commission by the contraction of traffic, others by the need to modernise, such as the previously mentioned dieselisation programme.

Now came the turn of the signalling. The old fashioned semaphore signals with an oil lamp at night had limitations and had become inadequate to cope with the faster trains now in use. The associated block telegraph signalling equipment was also outdated and far too cumbersome. The time taken by a signalman to tap out the code for a train and then to pull his levers was barely long enough to be able to handle steam hauled expresses at an average speed of sixty-five to seventy miles an hour. Diesels were now running up to one hundred miles an hour with faster speeds envisaged.

Modernisation of the signalling became a priority. Electric signals had long since proved their efficiency at Paddington and Bristol. Now with the benefit of modern electronics signals could be controlled from a long way off by a central signal box. This type of signal box, the first of which was built at Reading in 1965, controlled an area from the borders of Maidenhead to the east and to Didcot Foxhall junction in the west, was called a 'panel'. Covering an area of this extent required three signalmen and a supervisor. The layout of the track under its control was represented by a diagram on the angled desk in straight lines, together with signal indications and operating buttons. On the vertical panel above the layout is repeated with all the appropriate train information before the signalman.

Each signalman controls a certain section, the Didcot end man had full control of all the junctions in the area of Didcot. This is achieved by the use of a computer at Reading relaying information to its counterpart at Didcot which then operates the selected signals or points.

Signalmen operating this type of panel have no need to keep in contact with each other, as a train arrives within the area it is automatically described on the panel.

The signals are high intensity colour lights, capable of showing red, green, yellow or double yellow; the latter acting as an advanced indication of the single yellow ahead which warns of a red aspect beyond. The lamps have a double filament – should the main one fail, the secondary one, at a slightly lower wattage, automatically comes into operation. At the lower wattage the lamp is capable of maintaining the signal until the regular inspection is carried out. If the light in the red aspect fails altogether it automatically places the signal to its rear to red, as a precaution against the driver failing to notice a signal is missing.

The indication given by a signal is repeated on the panel in the form of a small light, but only displays red or green to indicate a stop or proceed aspect is being given by the signal. Any other aspect such as yellow, double yellow or a subsidiary signal on the same post also give the green proceed indication.

On each signal post there is a telephone with direct communication with the controlling signalman. At junctions such as Didcot all the signals are controlled by the signalman but automatically revert to red after the passing of a train. Between these controlled sections most of the signals are automatic in operation, being controlled by the passage of trains, automatically clearing to proceed as the line ahead becomes clear. The signalman is always aware of the position of trains in his area. When the line is clear the track indicator lights are out, but when he signals it for a train to proceed, the track shows a row of white lights. When a train moves onto the track which is signalled, the white lights are replaced by red lights until the whole of the train has moved from the track.

This advanced method of signalling sounded the death knell for what was unfortunately an outdated method of working. Unfortunate, because the railway as we knew it changed dramatically. Those gantries of signals we knew at the major junctions and even the lonely ones out in the country had for so long been part of the essence of the railway scene, were now extinct. Despite the efficiency of the new electric signals, they had no character, they all look alike, particularly to the driver, all set height and the same distance from the running line. The only exception is a signal requiring a position on a gantry.

Signalmen no longer see trains passing, the concentrated work which they now perform is all before them. The driver misses the friendly wave he was used to when passing the manual boxes.

Whilst many regret the loss of the Great Western and all it stood for, grudgingly accepting the new, it must be said that the new signalling with faster trains running on modern track does bring distant stations closer together, if only in time.

On 17 May 1965 all the manual boxes in the Reading and Didcot area were closed with the opening of the new panel box; a new era had begun.

It seemed that very little change could overcome the railway now, in fact great advances were made modernising the track. Many crossovers were taken out of the main lines, leaving only the barest of essential junctions. Between the crossovers remaining the track was laid as continuous welded rail without joints, only expansion joints to allow for variations of length due to temperature changes. Elaborate machines now lay and maintain the track to keep them in top condition.

The goods trains as we knew them also disappeared, trundling along as they did with a long train of wagons wobbling along behind, and the little guards van making up the rear.

Goods traffic and individual wagon loads had long since been falling off. In their place the new age of freight train was emerging; the block trains as they were known. Among the first of this type came the full load petrol trains running from Southampton via the branch line to Didcot and on to Birmingham. At first these trains were hauled by steam locos and later diesels took over the work, the usual type of diesel in use was supplied by the Southern Region, depending upon the weight of train a 65xx class diesel electric loco was at the head, but as the trains got heavier two of these locos coupled together in multiple became the norm. Also in the first instance these tank trains were vacuum braked. Within a short period of time new tank wagons were provided, fitted with compressed air brakes.

During the same period in the early part of 1968 the first of the newly designed freightliner vehicles came into service on the Western Region. These can only be described as an advanced design of the old GWR container principle with special flat wagons to carry the containers on. The new vehicles were designed with smaller wheels to allow for low loading, therefore larger containers. Three sizes were built, giving versatility to the use of the vehicles. Sets of three of these are permanently coupled with bar couplings, in the main, running as a train of fifteen. The normal speed was seventy-five mph, but with the new air brake there was no problem in braking the train, even at this very high speed and with a train weighing as much as 1,500 tons, three times that of the steam hauled passenger trains at a lower speed. Braking is constant whatever the weight of the train, each vehicle is fitted with a variable load valve to regulate the amount of brake individually according to the load it carries.

We have now reached the stage where all local passenger services are worked by DMUs, main line inter-city's by diesel locos and all freight trains hauled by diesels. The High Speed Trains, seeming at the time to be the ultimate expresses, now came on the scene. They arrived without much ado, we took them over, trained the drivers, and they went into service without a fanfare. There was of course some trepidation when first running at 125mph, wondering how well the braking would perform, but this had been taken care of with extensive trials. Once again the braking distance is always constant.

A new problem was raised with the introduction of the High Speed Train. Fears were raised as to the safety of passengers standing on platforms when a train passed through at 125mph. It was expected that people would be knocked over by the displacement of air.

The only station of any consequence to test the effect was Didcot. It was the only station with straight platforms on the stretch of line which had been upgraded for 125 running. The time taken by a high speed train to pass by is only 7.2 seconds, therefore with two trains passing each other at a combined speed of 250mph the time taken is 3.6 seconds. When the time taken is related to distance travelled it proves very little time is allowed for moving away.

HST prototype train 252 001 at Paddington during its trial period. The first 125mph tests were run on the Western Region between Pangbourne and Challow, the only stretch of line suitable at the time. *Author's collection*

Top:
'Turbo' diesel stopping passenger train on the down relief at Didcot ready to depart to Oxford 9 March 1993.

Middle:
HST 43070 is diverted via the station, working the 11.18am Bournemouth to Edinburgh through service, normally it traversed the avoiding line.

Left:
Diesel shunters 09101 and 08924 in the foreground, with EE diesels 37128 and 37278 at the rear, stand in the holding sidings where once there was a very busy yard.

Author's collection

To assess the effects, dummies were made and erected at various points along Didcot up main platform, and two trains were calculated to pass through the station at the same time. There was only the one HST at this time so a square fronted class 50 worked the down main train. The calculations proved to be correct, and after several trials with the dummies placed in different places, the conclusion was drawn that if passengers were kept at least six feet from the platform edge there would be no danger; hence the broad yellow line on the platforms.

One can stand on Didcot station these days and realise that those who knew it in the days of steam, and through the war years, when the whole area was alive with activity, will find it difficult to realise the changes which have taken place. Those milling passengers have gone, the commuter services are the mainstay, and the importance of the junction has lessened with the reduction of passengers needing to change trains. The relentless goods trains no longer trundle through, those which pass do so with speed, and are gone in no time at all.

The signal boxes have gone, together with the semaphore signals dotting the skyline. The transfer shed has left a vacant space and the most dominant feature of the railway complex, the provender mill, no longer exists. In their place there is now a large car park, made possible by filling in the reservoir. The car park was made to attract passengers to Didcot station from the surrounding area, leading to the re-naming of the station as Didcot Parkway. To enhance the station the whole frontage has been rebuilt, incorporating a new booking office and improved passenger facilities. In common with all other Western Region stations the station has now been classified as an open station. Tickets are examined on the trains which eliminates ticket collectors at the platform gates.

By comparison with the Didcot at which I first worked, the station and its surroundings have now become very uninteresting.

The ordnance depot site was acquired by the CEGB for a new power station. Building work commenced in 1965 and five years later, in September of 1970, the generators were ready to operate. The plant was designed to operate from coal fired furnaces, trains brought in coal from the northern collieries in specially designed railway wagons. The wagons are loaded at the pithead as the train moves slowly under the chutes, then makes its way to Didcot where the coal is discharged while the train moves over hoppers at a speed of half a mile an hour. When the train arrives inside the power station sidings it comes under the control of the CEGB control tower. From the tower the signals are operated in a similar manner to that of the railway, the controller is also responsible for operating all the conveyer belts which take the coal away, and for watching his indicators for any fault which may occur in the mechanism, any malfunction is liable to cause a severe blockage in the system.

These trains, operating as they do, travelling round a loop at the colliery and again at the power station, are officially recognised as Merry-Go-Round trains (MGR).

The train arrives at the power station discharge plant signal where it is held only long enough for the details of the load to be handed in. The signal is cleared and after the driver has set his controls to 'slow motion' he moves off through the discharge plant at the controlled speed of half a mile an hour. The locomotive is put on full power and with the aid of modern electronics the steady speed is maintained regardless of the weight of the train gradually diminishing.

The train first passes over a weighbridge to measure the total weight of each wagon, as the wagons pass through, a lineside arm strikes the safety catch of the discharge hopper, when a number of wagons are over the underground hopper their position is detected and all the wagon hoppers are opened simultaneously by a second set of arms. In a matter of about ten seconds a total of 50 tons of coal has been discharged. Down below, massive paddles scoop the coal onto moving belts to carry it away to the outside surge tower from where it either goes to the furnaces or is diverted to the stacking area. The empty wagons then have their hoppers automatically closed and the safety catch locked before passing over a second weighbridge.

Should a fault occur as the train passes through, the men watching the discharge from a platform above can operate an emergency stop signal; this indicates to the driver that he must stop immediately. At this slow speed the train is stopped within a few feet. A carriage and wagon examiner finally watches from a low level cabin to check that all hoppers have been correctly closed before the train is allowed to join the main line.

The number of trains arriving at the power station daily now varies according to requirements. Sometimes only three or four, at others twice that. At the height of coal burning as many as eighteen trains a day were arriving, requiring the use of the two discharge roads. Now the power station has been partially converted to oilburning, a train of oil tanks arrive as and when required, thus the activity within the power station has diminished as elsewhere.

I had the duty, as inspector, of accompanying the first train into the plant and overseeing the operation of the locomotive through the discharge plant, followed by the pleasure of a conducted tour of the items described. It was a most interesting and enlightening tour; vastly different from my first encounter with the ordnance depot.

The general activity around the Didcot of today has changed, the station, the yards and the loco shed are all somewhat muted, but surprisingly, the signalman from his remote position at Reading, controls, at this time, 327 passenger rated trains daily at Didcot Junction. In addition there are a number of freights, particularly in the night hours.

Seventy trains pass through without stopping on the down road while ninety actually call at the station and eight start from there.

In the up direction seventy seven pass through, with ninety stopping and eight starting.

Although this number of trains are dealt with, the station has no life, trains either pass through at such speed as to be almost unnoticed and those which do stop are less significant than the old steam engines. Today's trains are much faster and more comfortable, but far less interesting.

Didcot station as seen from the new overbridge to the car park. The station looks very desolate at this time but hundreds of trains stop or pass through each day.

Author's collection

The latest in modernisation at Didcot. This signal gantry will enable up trains to call at Didcot – stopping in the down relief platform and allow through services to pass on the up main. The train will then use the existing crossover to return to the main line.

Author's collection

The modern building of Didcot Parkway, far removed from its original facade. A bus waits to leave the forecourt as in earlier days.

Author's collection

This view of Didcot Power Station shows the major part of the loop line which circumnavigates the stacking area. *Courtesy Bill Butler*

58004 diesel electric loco pauses at the signal before entering the coal discharge plant at the power station. A water spray straddles the first wagon to help lay the dust. *Author's collection*

58004 emerges from the coal discharge plant at half a mile an hour approaching the electronic weighing machine. *Author's collection*

CHAPTER ELEVEN

Memories

Nothing much remains of Brunel's original station with the all-over roof, having been replaced in 1885, even now, very little of the replacement still stands. The down main platform buildings which were renewed after the fire only one year after rebuilding, no longer exist. Now, in its place stands a modern station building. The present buildings on the up relief platform date from the 1932 station rebuilding. The only buildings which are left of the station of 1885 are those on the island platform, serving passengers as refreshment rooms and waiting rooms. The station staff also occupy similar rooms at the west end of the same platform. These old buildings can be recognised by the wooden panelled walls and the fact that they are very narrow.

Almost everything has been swept away in the name of progress, few records remain and in most cases only memories.

During my days at Didcot I had the privilege of working with most of the older drivers on odd occasions, particularly when covering spare duties. They all, without exception, related stories of how the railway used to be, carrying on with their work as if still in the past. Always they hinted, and often said, that times were much better for me than for them, they were probably right in many ways.

They usually referred back to how hard it was in their early days, some of them going back as far as the turn of the century, believing in the old cliche that they were the good old days, but even so relating the tortuous nature of the work, of the hardships they suffered through lack of weather protection, of the ten hours a day they were required to work and many other minor inconveniences, such as having to carry out some repairs to engines such as piston and valve spindle gland packing, which they considered was fitters work. Such was the antiquated methods still in use at Didcot at this time; no other shed did anything of this nature.

There was one such man who was able to recall many memories, Bill Inge, now a centenarian. I had never spoken to him since leaving Didcot in January 1946 until late 1988 when he was approaching his ninety-ninth birthday.

His memory was such that when I first made contact with him by phone I said:

'Hello Bill, I'm Jack Gardner. I don't suppose you will

remember me. I came to Didcot from Worcester at the start of the war.'

With hardly a pause he replied:

'Yes, I remember you. You worked with Bert East on the pilots.'

After a short conversation he invited me to call upon him to talk about old times; a date was fixed.

When I arrived Bill met me at the door. I introduced myself by saying:

'I'm Jack Gardner.'

After a short pause to gaze at me he said:

'Ah, I see now. My eyes are not so good these days, have to look a bit closer.'

'Come on in. I've just been doing a bit of cooking, see what I've been at.'

Bill proceeded to tell me of how he managed to take care of himself since his wife's death.

'Might as well as long as I can do it, mightn't I. It's a bit of an effort like, when you come to think of it, it's ninety-nine that I'm going.' Then after a short pause he added, 'It's better than going to the shops for it.'

Being at a loss for words I commented, 'You'll soon be getting a telegram from the Queen then Bill.'

He nodded in a matter of fact way.

'I suppose so.'

After a few more thoughtful moments Bill remembered his garden and talked on the subject for some considerable time, telling of how well his crops had always grown and the general interest in gardening; reminiscent of the topic of conversation so often carried on in the enginemen's cabin. Every railwayman in the town was proud of his garden. The interest in gardens developed mainly from the need to grow their own vegetables but also from the fact that the irregular turns of duty left little time to pursue other interests.

After some time dwelling on Bill's personal life I thought it time to broach the subject of the railway. I asked:

'How long is it that you have retired from work now Bill.'

'Do you mean from the railway?' After another thoughtful moment he continued, 'We'll take it from when I left school at eleven. I had what was called a workers certificate, to allow me to go to work.'

Bill related how it was necessary for him to leave school early in order to help support a rather large family. He moved from job to job, each time bettering his position until he made friends with a young man who was a fireman on the little branch line from Uffington to Faringdon, which was Bill's home. The young fireman suggested that Bill should go to Swindon and apply for a cleaners job. Bill said:

'I borrowed a bike and rode into Swindon on the Saturday morning. Old Lewis was the foreman there, I asked him if there was a chance of a job and he said, "Yes, start on Monday." Simple as that, and that's what I did.'

'Didn't he want a reference or medical then Bill?'

'No, he said, that will come later. I went back to my boss and he offered me an extra shilling a week to stay, to make it up to ten shillings a week. What, I said, the railway are paying me two shillings above that, and that's a lot of money.' He then added 'Yes my Christ, that's a lot of money my boy, and I'll tell you I went on and was made a fireman at that.'

'How long were you a cleaner then Bill, do you remember? '

'Who'er', he replied hesitatingly. 'Not long, because I went to Landore when I was seventeen.'

'So it was only a year at the most as a cleaner then.'

'Oh yes, not a twelve month, I was turned sixteen when I went down there, and from there I came to Landore. It was the time you had to shift for third class firing, and there was a chap who used to live in old Didcot but I can't remember his name now. He was made a third class fireman and sent to Landore and I was sent to Didcot to take his place. I was about seventeen and a half then, summut like that see. Came up here and been here ever since. War broke out and I was made a fireman, and then I was made an engineman.'

'Was that at the start of the war when you were made an engineman then Bill?'

'Yes, I was made an engineman during the war, the first war, and been here ever since. Then I had the misfortune to lose the sight of this eye.'

'How did that happen. Was it an accident at work?'

'It was shingles. They gave me a job in the office to keep me at work.'

'This is the Second World War now?', I queried.'I can remember working with you on the passengers before this happened to you.'

'Yes, because I had got up to my passenger work. They wanted to put me on the yard pilots but I was not satisfied with that, so I packed the job in.'

Bill left the railway at sixty-three with much regret. I asked him if he ever regretted starting work on the railway.

'No, no. I never regretted starting on the railway. There's one thing always in my mind on the railway Jack. You never knew it; a driver I fired to on the second class, he was as eccentric as the eccentrics on an engine he was, you never knew a man like him. We were going on the down Warwick, it was a double-home job. Ted Weaver was

his name and I want to tell you something about him. He turned to me and I thought he was going to say something about my work, but he said, "Do you know that the railway company lends me this engine to do my work." My God, that has stuck in me, but it's real isn't it. What the old boy said was right you know. When a man had his own engine that was it, wasn't it?'

'They used to go down there on a Sunday morning and on top of the dome there was a lubricating valve, they used to take that down when the engine was cold to put a few drops of oil down there for the regulator. Every Sunday morning when he was at home he would do that.'

'Well, I expect it was before your time, but you never knew Jack Hanniford down there.'

'I'm afraid that was long before my time but I've heard tell of him.'

'He was a second class man about the time I was talking about now, when I was firing to Ted Weaver at the time. He had a fireman with him, Bill Peters, and I always said that if I had a driver like that I would never work with him. He never knew what it was like to come to work sober. That kiddy, Bill Peters, had a heart of gold. He took that bloke to Stourbridge and Bristol and all over the ruddy show, when he's hardly been able to stand up on the footplate. He came to him one night, six o'clock at night we used to go out for Stourbridge, and before they left the yard old Jack Hanniford, he called that kid everything from a dog to a devil. Do you know what he did? He stepped off the engine. He said."I won't go out with you", and he walked back to the shed and he wouldn't go out. Did you know what they did to Jack Hanniford? They put him down to Swindon firedropping. There were some hard men to get on with but thank goodness not many like that.'

That punishment was typical of the draconian attitude of those days.

'Unfortunately Bill, we all had to concede that the driver was the boss, but I'm sure that in my time things had changed for the better.'

'I worked with such a man for about a year, he made my life very miserable indeed for most of the time we were together at work, but when we were travelling home, or even if we met in the club, he couldn't do enough for me. I learned to live with it, always believing it was the tension of the job which caused the irritation.'

Bill said, 'I know who you mean, he was an awkward devil.'

'The first man I fired to here was George Bowering. You didn't know him either.'

'Wasn't there a George Bowering who kept the petrol station? '

'Yes, that's it, that's him.'

'I remember him at the petrol station but not on the railway.'

'He was an awkward man at the best of times, but at work he was a damn sight worse than that. Well at that time you were beholden to them, weren't you. After we had a severe quarrel and I threatened him with the coal

London & West of England Express.

Memories are made of this! A 'Saint' class stands in the down Oxford branch highlighting the curvature of the line prior to the 1932 station rebuilding. From this platform the train could depart either to Oxford or return to the main line for the west.

Author's collection

pick he was never so bad. Later, at the petrol station, he was good to me, damn nice in fact. It's like you said, the job got them down a bit.'

'I suppose, Bill, you can remember the ten hour day. You used to work ten hour rosters and much more at times I believe.'

'I had twelve hours a day alright and twelve bob a week for a very long time. Twelve hours a day when I was cleaning, so I was made a fireman with no rise.'

'So there's the difference Bill. When I started in 1936 the pay was twenty four shillings a week for six days of eight hours.'

'Which year did you start Bill?'

'I was born in 1889, so it was 1900 when I first started work and I was seventeen when I came here. I've got a trunk upstairs with the date on it. Always kept it packed with things in case they decided to send me somewhere to another depot. They did in those days you know.'

Moving away from Bill's own memories I asked if he could remember a small gantry of three signals which were in the provender mill sidings and worked independently from the signalbox. His eyesight prevented him from seeing much of the picture which I had shown him, but he was able to explain:

'Now I've got a faint recollection of that. I'll tell you what, there's three roads in the provender stores. Those signals were for those roads, so that nothing could move while the men were working on the vehicles inside the building.'

'Do you remember a driver named Fisher at Didcot? I knew his son who worked in the transfer shed offices. He understood that was the reason for the signals.'

'Yes I can remember his father, Ernie was his name, somewhere to my age and seniority.'

'I can also remember him from working with him. He was one of the old brigade who treated all his firemen with respect and consideration.'

There followed an interesting review of the farmers who had benefited by the provender stores with Bill remembering that 'Campbell was the man in charge of the provender stores when I first came here.' He next recalled a vivid account of a very unusual incident at Didcot:

'Don't know whether you've heard of it or not. I forget the name of the bloke who was inspector on the platform at the time. Well I was going to tell you this. One year there was a train starting from here, well it used to start from Oxford at two o'clock and we went through to Winchester and then came back with the goods. Well this Saturday, I can't tell you the two teams now but one of them was Wolverhampton, was playing in the cup final at Wembley. I forget which month it actually was now, somewhere near the break of the summer, about the beginning of June time, playing in the cup final in brilliant sunshine. We had a snowstorm here just as the three o'clock was about to leave. You know how far the three o'clock went? It pulled up round the corner over the Hagbourne Road bridge, couldn't get no farther. It stopped

there until Sunday morning. I believe the people who kept the hotel opposite was Perry, in any case they also had the license for the railway refreshment rooms. Neither he, the station master or the station inspector went to see how the passengers were. They all knew the train was snowed in but didn't bother. They sacked the inspector and shifted the station master for leaving those people marooned all that time. Now that was in my time!'

Bill continued with a lengthy reminiscence of all his contemporaries, finishing with the comment, 'I don't feel my age you know. The doctor comes to see me once a month. If I'd got a better pair of legs, I've had them a long time. They've done good service haven't they. When I started on the footplate you know, they were steel plates, no wooden floorboards then, but later they got round to putting a piece of wood on them. But they didn't reckon, and you can remember this, they didn't give the enginemen any cover did they.'

'I suppose you can remember some of the older engines with only a weather board for protection.'

'Coming up from Stourbridge or Wolverhampton on a winter's night your old eyelids were frozen, you'd soon poke your head back inside. We had to work with our overcoats on when it was like that, expect you had to do at times as well.'

'Yes Bill I've done quite a bit of that.'

'As I was saying, I don't feel my age. I don't feel as though I'm coming up to ninety-nine. Whether that's a good or bad thing I don't know.'

Bill was probably the oldest Great Western footplate man able to recount these sort of tales. A man with many fond memories.

Other aspects of Didcot are also worth remembering, such as the thoughts of a lady who wrote of her early experiences. In an article for a local newspaper she writes:

...when we arrived in April of 1915 and found the place almost unbearable, but as we had to live here, some of the railwaymen of that time set to work, and they formed a Trades Labour Council which got a good many things moving. My husband was secretary and kept a huge pile of records which unfortunately I did not keep. There were parish councillors who could not write their own name, who opposed everything that these few railwaymen wanted to do; this, before they got things going was what Didcot was like. No depot, no council houses, no lighting, no electricity, no hot and cold water, no hospital, no resident doctor, no nurse and no chemists shop. These few people, myself included, were positively hated by the few inhabitants of this place. I well remember no chemists shop, when I had my baby I had to go to Oxford to get things for him.

The inference is that the lady's husband was a railwayman and that they most likely lived in Northbourne where the railwaymen in general were shunned by the local population.

This does show that Didcot was a rather desolate place, but there was a little ray of light, if only from the railway lamps in Station Hill.

The three smaller towns in Berkshire which had each opposed the railway were now left without its benefits, each in their own way regretting their short-sighted approach, requesting a rail link.

Henley, Wantage, Wallingford and Abingdon-which lost its status as the county town – remain as they had always been, small market towns. Reading, by comparison, after some fierce arguments, eventually welcomed the railway and prospered.

It must be said that Reading was in an ideal situation from the onset, being sighted at the confluence of the Kennet & Avon canal with the Thames, and also being on the main stage-coach route from London to Bristol. The river distance from Reading to London is seventy two miles, whereas by rail it is exactly half that. It was only a matter of time before Reading became the county town of Berkshire at the expense of Abingdon.

Henley was connected to the main line by a four and half mile branch line 1 June 1857; incidentally to be the first line to be fitted with the GWR automatic train control.

The Wallingford branch of three and a quarter miles opened 2 July 1866.

Wantage never had a direct connection with the main line, but benefited from a private tramway which ran alongside the road for two miles into the good yard at Wantage Road station.

The Abingdon branch of a little under two miles opened 2 June 1856 and connected with the main line at a point a quarter of a mile north of the Thames bridge at Nuneham. The station was named Abingdon Junction, later re-located at Radley, and the branch line extended to the new station.

Brunel's plan to locate the junction at Didcot did little to aid the local population. Didcot failed to grow in prosperity, and development was slow. Its remoteness, without any good trunk roads near, left it isolated. The railway by-passing the village as it did for five years prior to the building of the station did nothing to help. Had it not been for the need of railway workers the village might well have remained undeveloped.

From the railway point of view the importance of the junction has always been recognised. The loco shed, renewed for the second time, and being one of the latest on the Great Western, is the only one still in existence and still being used as a loco shed, maintaining the tradition of the Great Western Railway.

There are other memories, which from some aspects should be forgotten, but nevertheless form a part of the Didcot scene.

Accidents have occurred in the area in recent years prompting remarks in newspapers, such as, 'What's wrong with Didcot?'

Speculation by the press would have us believe there was something inherently amiss with the track or signalling in the area, and that all the incidents were related.

It was not a bit like that, each accident had a different set of circumstances; they just happened to be at Didcot.

All accidents are regrettable, particularly those which involve life and limb. From my railway inspector's viewpoint they need to be remembered for the purpose of making every endeavour to prevent a repetition.

The first fatal accident happened at Appleford Crossing soon after midnight on 14 November 1942 when a government stores train from the ordnance depot became de-railed. The subsequent pile up of wagons engulfed the 'midnight' passenger train which had just left the avoiding line heading for Oxford and the north. The stores train locomotive – a 'Saint' class 4-6-0 – turned over onto its side, killing both men. In addition two other railwaymen who were travelling in the front guards van of the passenger train were also killed and a number of passengers were injured.

The tragedy was caused by an error on the part of the driver who had misread the signals at Didcot North junction. He was under the impression that the clear signals shown for the express were his and proceeded as if on the main line. He was in fact signalled via the down goods loop as far as Appleford Crossing, where the line terminated.

A very serious accident occurred at Milton, about a mile to the west of Didcot, on 22 November 1955 when a 'Britannia' class Pacific No.70026 *Polar Star* with a Cardiff to Paddington train left the line. The passenger train had been diverted to the up goods loop to by-pass engineering work on the up main line. The driver had failed to recognise that he was being turned into the loop, even though he had passed a caution distant signal at Steventon. The locomotive passed over the crossover points at too great a speed, became de-railed and toppled down the high embankment, taking a number of coaches with it. Eleven passengers were killed and another 157 injured.

On 14 August 1964 in the early hours of the morning, a loaded petrol train running from Fawley to Bromford Bridge came into collision with a light engine at North Junction.

The light engine had left Oxford shed to work a train forward to the north from Didcot. Arriving at North box on the west curve the signalman stopped the driver with a red light from his box to arrange where the loco was going. He then instructed the driver to go back over the points to be turned into the yard. 'Back' to the signalman meant back with the engine and as the engine had arrived running backwards, i.e. tender first, the signalman intended it to carry on that way. The driver took the message as meaning him to go back over the points the way he had arrived and then into the yard from there. The driver reversed his engine and proceeded back the way he had just come.

In the meantime the signalman had signalled the loaded tank train across the junction from the avoiding line, with the result that the light engine collided with it causing it to catch fire. The ferocity of the fire completely ruined a large number of tanks, the footbridge over the line was

Fire blackened ex LMS 8F, condemned following its disastrous collision with a petrol train at Didcot North junction.

J R Fairman

buckled beyond repair and the loco, a Midland Region 8F No.48734 was towed to Didcot shed from where it was taken for scrap.

On 27 September 1967 the 9.45am Paddington to Bristol with nine coaches headed by diesel loco 'Warship' D853 *Thruster* became de-railed at Foxhall junction.

The train had been diverted to the down relief line at Reading West junction. At Didcot, the driver, who was not very well acquainted with the route, travelled through the crossovers at the termination of the relief line at Foxhall at a speed too high for the junction. This caused a whiplash effect at the rear of the train as it sped across the two crossover leads, causing the coaches at the rear to become de-railed. One passenger died and there were 23 injured.

There was also a de-railment in the up goods loop at Foxhall in the early hours of one winter. An Oxford driver had relieved a freight train at Swindon. He was unaware

at the time that the locomotive had been converted to a dual-braked loco, that is, the same brake handle operating either a vacuum or an air brake, he was not fully trained in its use. He departed Swindon around midnight with the Brush diesel class 47 and a full load and had an uninterrupted run until he was signalled into the up goods loop at Steventon. From here the driver allowed the train to run freely on the slight down gradient but was unable to bring the train to a stop at Foxhall, subsequently being de-railed by the catch point at the end of the loop.

The resulting wreckage blocked the junction for two days but no one was injured.

Other unfortunate incidents have occurred in the area but none of them related. The MAS signalling system has an excellent safety record, the track is modern and the trains, together with the braking system, are of the highest standard. Hopefully there will be no more such memories.

CHAPTER TWELVE

Great Western Preservation

The development of Didcot had progressed hand in hand with the railway for many years, going along at a leisurely pace. Until now its destiny had been guided by the railway to some extent and also by the military. Rationalisation of the railway brought a new outlook and with it came severe job losses, and a tremendous reduction in the number of men employed on the railway, there was a virtual parting of company. The importance of the railway diminished, as far as the local community was concerned. It was no longer a prime employer in the district.

The hustle and bustle of the steam shed ceased when diesel locomotives were introduced, together with the diesel units working the local passenger services.

Many reductions were made, the saddest of all, to the steam enthusiasts, was the demise of the steam locomotives, and the closing of the shed. Diesels were arriving in ever increasing numbers and, surprisingly, attracting a great deal of interest, but even so, the dying steam was being mourned by the faithful. Train spotters were out as much as ever to tick off the diesel numbers in their little books, but for that reason only, otherwise the diesel had no real attraction. Few of these enthusiasts were nostalgic about the passing of steam.

There was, however, a small band of schoolboy spotters who spent a considerable amount of time using the footbridge over the east end of the station at Southall as a vantage point to watch and record steam engines. Quite a good position it was, with all types of locomotives and trains passing beneath in a regular procession. Fast trains dashed up and down the main line to and from Paddington whilst the relief lines were occupied mainly by stopping passenger trains and goods trains of all types. At certain times of the day auto trains were in service, completing the variety.

The shunting yards to the east and to the west were also in good view, together with the branch line to Brentford Docks; enough to get any young man excited.

These young men were among the minority who could perceive that Dr Beeching's cuts could take away all that they held dear. They were not appeased by the knowledge that the British Transport Commission (BTC) had issued a list of locomotives to be preserved as static exhibits for posterity.

It was real live locos which they were interested in. They talked, no doubt ambiguously at the time, about buying one of the locos not listed for preservation. Keeping their feet on the ground, although their heads were in the clouds, they opted to make an effort to purchase one of the fascinating little 'Auto' engines which were so prominent at Southall, and which I had much pleasure working on as a driver at Southall.

It was late in 1961 when a small committee was formed with the serious intention of raising money for the project by placing an advertisement in the *Railway Magazine* asking for subscriptions towards purchasing a 48xx 0-4-2T.

The inaugural meeting was held at Southall in May 1962 at which new members were accepted and the name Great Western Preservation Society was adopted with the sole aim of preserving what they could of the GWR.

Others joined and soon there was a team of very knowledgeable men who produced their first newsletter in March 1963. In June 1963 the word preservation was dropped from the title, settling the name as Great Western Society. Also during 1963 two of this type of engine were offered to the society, numbers 1450 and 1466, the society opted for the latter at a price of £750 in February of 1964. Although the engine was in full working order, the railway would only deliver it to the goods yard at Totnes, a long way from where the dream started. They had no choice but to accept this offer, but fortune favoured them. Through the old pals act, they were able to take up an offer by a private industrial company to stable the loco in its sidings; at least it had a home for a while.

The following month a number of these founder members journeyed to Totnes with the intention of cleaning their new acquisition. Seeing it working was not on the agenda, just the pleasure of getting it looking as new as possible. Their enthusiasm overtook them with the result that the fire was lit and in what must have seemed an eternity, steam was raised. The intrepid bunch could not contain themselves and tentatively taught themselves the rudiments of driving, although I suspect that some, if not all, had previously inveigled their way onto footplates at some time or other. Under these auspicious circumstances No.1466 moved under its own power at the hands of the society for the first time. It's just as well that all went right or there may not have been a society today.

At this time the following of the society was small in number, the bulk of the steam enthusiasts were too busy riding behind the remaining steam engines while they still had the opportunity to do so. To these people it was more important than concerning themselves with preservation. Perhaps they thought there was no hope, considering the attitude of the BTC.

Those who had faith put all their energies into fund raising with the firm belief that one day soon their efforts would be rewarded. As time went by they also realised that locomotives were not the only things needing preserving and turned their minds to even greater efforts to raise money for rolling stock, and any other item which constituted a part of the Great Western.

The main aim at this time was to purchase a trailer for the auto engine. This was more in keeping with the working which first inspired the venture. Other coaches and rolling stock were later acquired, and even more tendered for, but there was still no place where they could run them.

In 1964 the society got recognition from BR who allowed it to organise a rail tour from Swindon via Westbury to Bristol and return.

By now the society was growing at a much greater rate, doubling its membership and creating a much greater interest in its activities. Several groups were formed throughout the Great Western system, each contributing to the society whatever they could lay their hands on. Money raising was the order of the day, it was essential to obtain as much of the Great Western as possible before it all went to scrap, indeed, it was the scrapheap where a considerable amount of the purchases were eventually made.

As the stock grew in numbers the sidings at Totnes became too full, preventing movements of the stock, a new venue was sorely needed.

The Reading group, who were now using Taplow for their meetings prompted consideration as to whether this site could be the answer to the accommodation problem. Arrangements were in hand to run the auto engine and trailer on the Dart Valley Railway and when Nos.7808 and 6106 were privately purchased the society had the task of managing them. To enable the society to accommodate them at Totnes, two small locos and three coaches were transferred to Buckfastleigh.

The society was anxious to own one of the GWR mixed traffic engines of the 4-6-0 classes, and asked members to vote on which type they would prefer; the options being a 'Hall', 'Grange', or 'Manor'. The vote was overwhelmingly in favour of a 'Hall'. A separate fund was started specially for this purpose and extra efforts were put into raising the capital. Eventually No.6998 *Burton Agnes Hall* was selected and an offer of £2,500 was made to the BTC and duly accepted.

The loco made its last run for BR on 3 January 1966 and was then taken out of service to become the property of the Great Western Society. The loco was in full working order and in April of that year ran under its own power to Totnes to be handed over.

GWS preserved loco No.6998 *Burton Agnes Hall* at Worcester Shrub Hill station on 24 June 1973 after working from Didcot with a train of enthusiasts for Hereford.

Author's collection

Through the good offices of the Reading group an open day was arranged at Taplow for 15 September 1966. Short rides were laid on in one of the restored Ocean Saloons hauled by No.6106. A special event of the day was the arrival of 7808 *Cookham Manor* hauling a train of enthusiasts from Birmingham. The day was a tremendous success, convincing the society more than ever that a larger site was needed.

The loco shed at Didcot had been closed for two years and all eyes were on it. The question was being asked. What if it could be used to house the now vast amount of locos and rolling stock in the hands of the society? The possibilities were endless. The shed was almost new, having been built only thirty five years previously and still containing all the ancillary equipment intact. The shed, one of the latest to be built by the Great Western, had deep pits, all the offices and stores were available together with the various mess rooms. The lifting shop was still in working order, also the elevated coal stage with the water tank on top to supply the columns on all the roads. Who could wish for anything better?

Needless to say no effort was spared to gain the sole use of such an establishment. Eventually the society was able to win over BR and was granted the full use of the shed and its equipment. Unfortunately BR had removed one item of importance. The 65ft turntable had been removed by them soon after the closure of the shed, at this stage its loss was not important.

In November of 1967, following another successful open day at Taplow at which an even greater number of locos and vehicles were on show, preparations were made to move into the newly acquired premises. Engine No.6106 did a round up of all outlying vehicles from Kensington, Taplow and Oxford to haul them to their new home at Didcot on 4 November. It was early December before the remainder of the society's stock was collected from various points in Devon. The train was hauled by No.6998 *Burton Agnes Hall*, one of the society's own engines with No.1466 in steam in the train.

Although it has been mentioned that the shed was intact and in a good condition it took the society several years to make good the dilapidation caused by previous years of neglect, both by BR in the years of running down and the years of emptiness. The enginemen were still required to use the offices to book on and off duty with the mess room being the only section maintained.

The euphoria at acquiring the site was only matched by the enthusiasm of the members, they were well aware of the work ahead but nothing could make them flinch from the ambitions they had set themselves. There were unforseen snags, such as the problem of open day visitors having to cross the BR carriage sidings to get to the site. Because of this safety aspect the MOT were involved and needed to be satisfied that everything was arranged in a safe manner. There was the need to contain visitors within the boundary of the shed and sidings, and fencing became a high priority. Safe walkways had to be provided and adequate insurance cover supplied. To sum it up, it was not an easy proposition to get to grips with in a short time. The increasing numbers of new and dedicated workers revelled in the challenge, as subsequent results have shown.

Then came the other problem of steaming the locos on BR property. The society came under the same stringent control of the MOT as did BR. Members were well aware of the regulations regarding care and examination of boilers from their previous experiences and also knew about the implications attached to the mechanical maintenance from when they worked their train from Devon.

MOT regulations forbade them from operating their own locos on BR territory, making it necessary to employ BR drivers and firemen to operate within their compound. In addition a BR loco inspector had to be on site to oversee all movements. Quite often two sets of men were needed with the railway charging the society for their use. In addition the inspector's salary helped to make a drain on their resources. The shed movements were normally carried out at weekends for the purpose of placing locos and stock in position for the working staff. As time passed the shunting took on a new interest when we formed up a train of the society's own preserved coaches for an enthusiasts' special, hauled by two of the society's preserved locos, No.7808 and No.6998 with the 'Vintage' train on 14 June 1975. I had the pleasure and the honour of accompanying No.7808 at the head of the train, a very satisfying trip.

No.6998 was the first of the restored locos to venture out, but although it had undergone severe boiler and mechanical inspection by BR inspectors it failed to perform to the best standards expected, gremlins had crept in. Unfortunately on its second attempt a steam pipe failure resulted in assistance home by a diesel loco, not a very happy sight. There was frustration all round, but downhearted, no, just a greater challenge.

The next trip proved to be a great success when the loco ran via Banbury to Stratford-upon-Avon with flying colours. I was fortunate on this occasion also to be accompanying the footplate crew. We encountered a slight problem on the outward journey with a lubricator condensing steam pipe leak in the cab. The steam condensing in the cab roof caused very uncomfortable conditions, water dripped all over us.

When the train was stabled in Long Marston sidings one of the accompanying, very dedicated, fitters worked hard at it and after what seemed a rather long time succeeded in making a good repair. The run home was first class and we were able to boast right time all the way, out and back. Proof that restored engines can be relied upon to do a good job. This was to be the first of many successful main line runs.

As other locos were restored they were put out on main line trains to show themselves off to the thousands of enthusiasts who forever flock to vantage points alongside the track with their cameras. There was a fantastic number out to watch the Vintage train pass by double-headed.

The scene at Didcot GWS on a rainy day with most of the visitors taking cover.

Author's collection

Wantage Tramway No.5 *Shannon* stands idle at the rear of the shed.

Author's collection

Bonnie Prince Charlie showing off its paces on an open day.   *Author's collection*

A new arrival on a low loader waiting to be lifted off.   *Author's collection*

GWR diesel rail car No.22 on the demonstration line.
Merchant Navy Locomotive Preservation Society

BR 9F 2-10-0 privately owned as *Black Prince*, at Oxford, having departed Didcot GWS to work forward an enthusiasts special. *Author's collection*

No.7808 *Cookham Manor* and No.6998 *Burton Agnes Hall* head back to Didcot passing Cropedy with a special to and from Birmingham on 6 October 1979.

Author's collection

It had become commonplace to see the society's restored locos out in pairs with any permutation of the four usual ones; Nos.7808 *Cookham Manor*; 6998 *Burton Agnes Hall*; 5900 *Hinderton Hall*, and 5051 *Drysllwyn Castle/Earl Bathurst* as it was renamed in June 1936. As reward for the hard work and dedication of the men who had made this possible, they each in turn were allowed a short ride on the footplate when the locos worked the specials. The actual working of the engines was always in the hands of BR men.

Under MOT regulations restored engines were limited to sixty miles an hour, even though they were up to the same standard as those coming out of Swindon factory as new. It was my policy to stick to this restriction, but no doubt it got 'bent' at times.

Probably one of the most important milestones in the history of the society was when it was eventually granted autonomy. It was then able to run all its business within its compound without any interference from BR. The society trained its own drivers and guards, shunters and operating staff. The drivers and guards were examined by BR inspectors on the locos and the applicable rules.

This accomplished, they were able to run trains on the demonstration roads for the benefit of visitors who also had the pleasure of rides in the trains, something many youngsters have never done before.

Their newly found freedom also allowed them to manage the weekend shunting which unfortunately made my colleagues and myself redundant, much to my regret.

The society had many ambitious plans for the future, fund raising was stepped up and various schemes were invented to part people from their money in a good cause.

The various groups which had been formed throughout the Great Western sysrern contributed many items of interest, such as old wagons which had been virtually left to rot away, and dilapidated old coaches which had seen their days out as chalet homes for summer breaks by a river somewhere. Some of these were recovered from the most difficult places by the intrepid rescuers. Probably the most interesting and important find was by the Taunton group, when they discovered sections of original Brunel broad gauge track complete with points and crossovers. This has become a marvellous complement to the transfer shed which has been re-erected within the site – a Brunel structure complete with track preserved for posterity.

Numerous other items have been collected for the relics museum, many of which are on permanent display. Every possible type of vehicle has been gathered together, some forty-odd coaches, about thirty goods wagons, a breakdown train of four vehicles, three cranes and several more recent vehicles.

This fine array is complemented by an excellent collection of twenty three locomotives, plus three diesel locomotives, two of which are ex BR diesel hydraulics, the other a small shunter.

To complete the scene two signal boxes have been acquired and put into use operating a variety of signals.

Additional interest is given by regular visits of other famous locomotives. Possibly the most apt was the replica of the *Iron Duke* running on broad gauge track hauling replica broad gauge coaches, reflecting more than anything else what it was really like.

The Great Western Society's museum is a venue where all the family can enjoy a visit, and where men can become boys again, and where I can also relive my own lifetime on the footplate.

The dreams of those few schoolboys were more far reaching than they could possibly have anticipated. From the humble beginning with No.1466 there now stands a monument to Brunel and the Great Western Railway.

Men and Moguls – from Great Western Railway to Great Western Society. **Left:** Didcot footplatemen – Jim East, driver, with fireman Doug Morton – wait in the bay at Reading after working the 5.35pm Didcot ordnance depot workers train.

Right: The author stands beside Mogul No.5322 at Didcot GWS, with the tender proudly displaying **GREAT WESTERN**.

Doug Morton
Author's collection

An aerial view of Didcot station and the Great Western Society's complex, with the avoiding line sweeping away to the right.

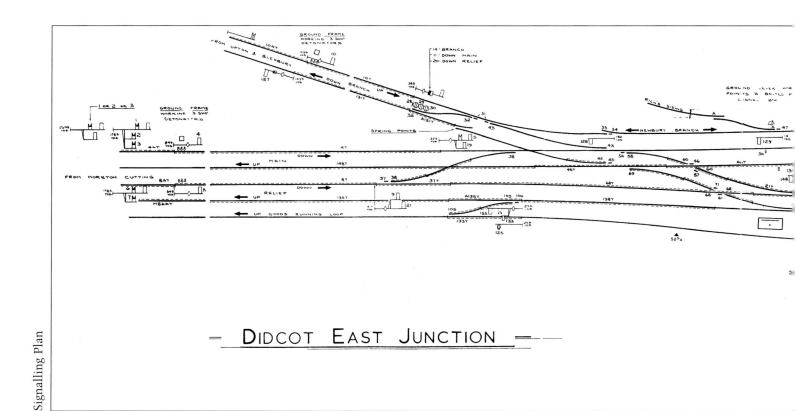

= DIDCOT EAST JUNCTION =

= DIDCO

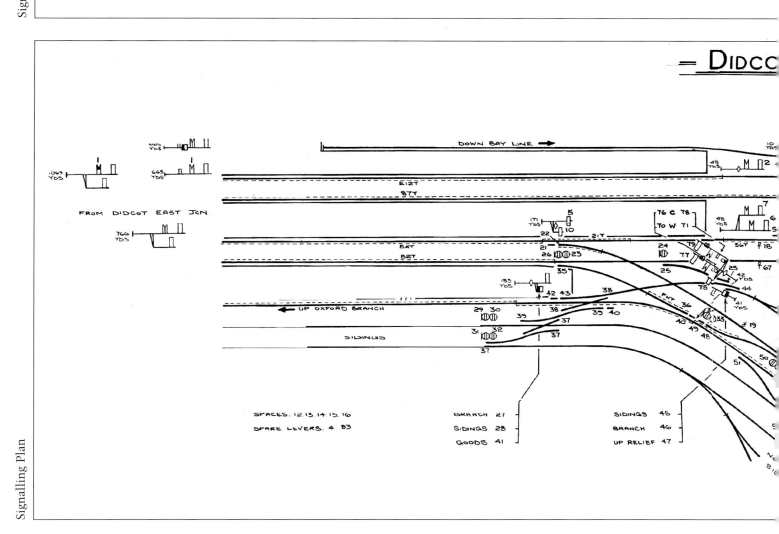

SPACES. 12.13.14.15.16

SPARE LEVERS. 4. 83

BRANCH 27

SIDINGS 28

GOODS 41

SIDINGS 45

BRANCH 46

UP RELIEF 47

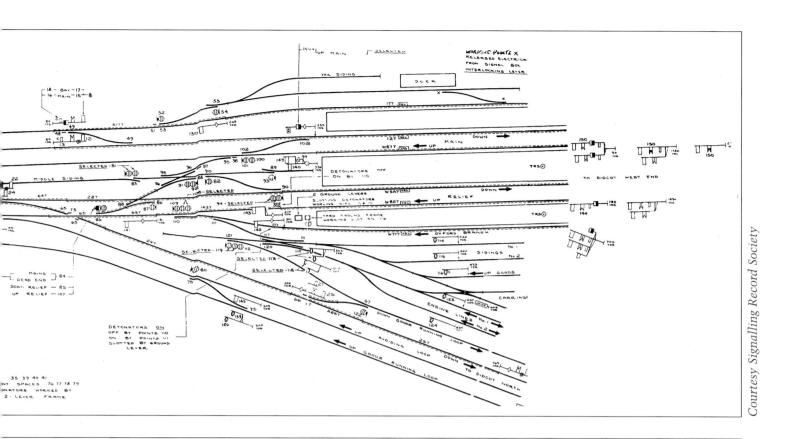

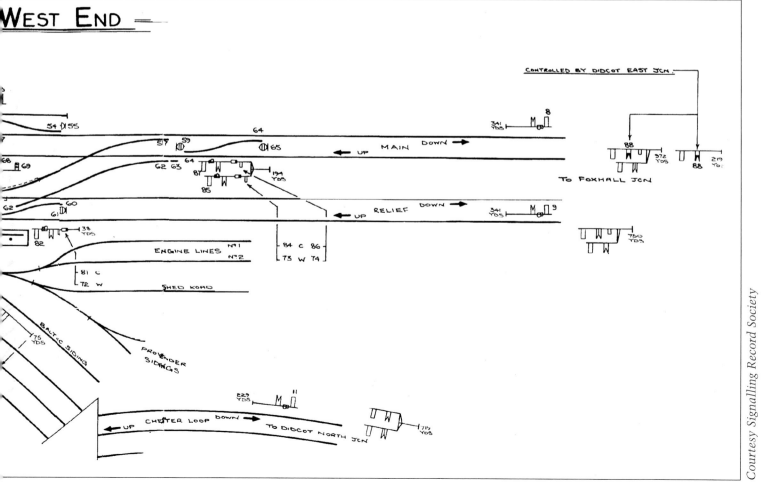

WEST END

Courtesy Signalling Record Society

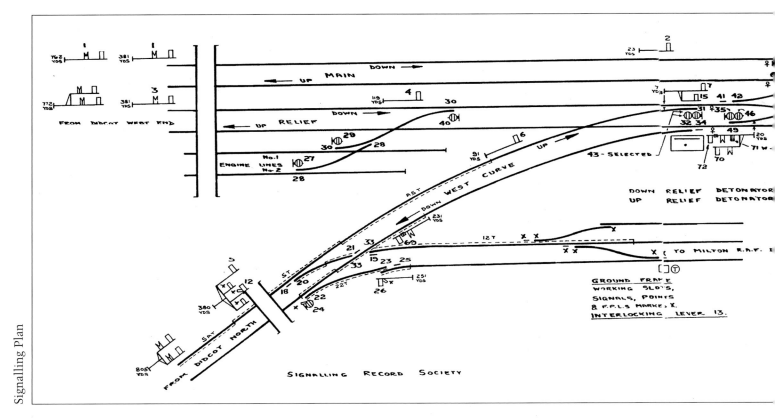

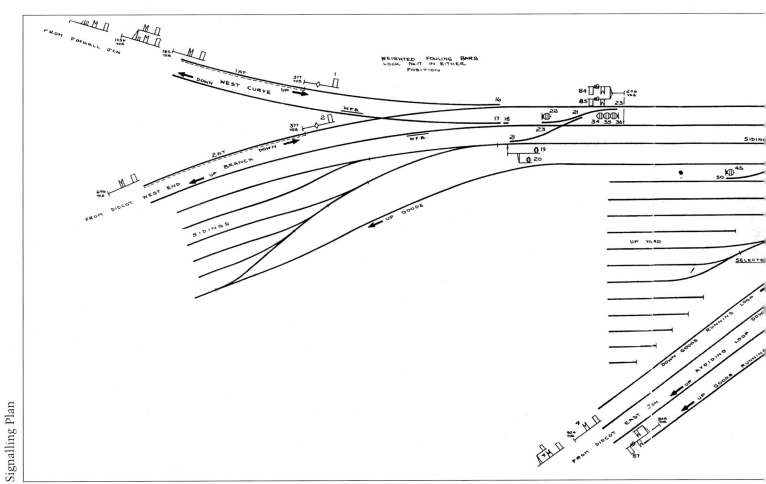

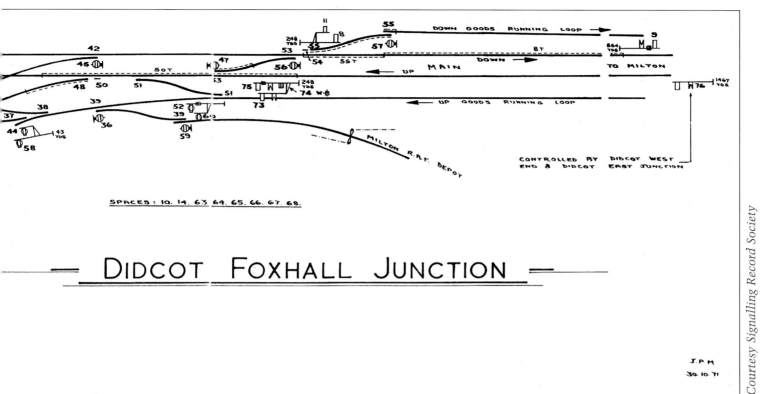

— DIDCOT FOXHALL JUNCTION —

SPACES: 10. 14. 63. 64. 65. 66. 67. 68.

J.P.M
30.10.71

Courtesy Signalling Record Society

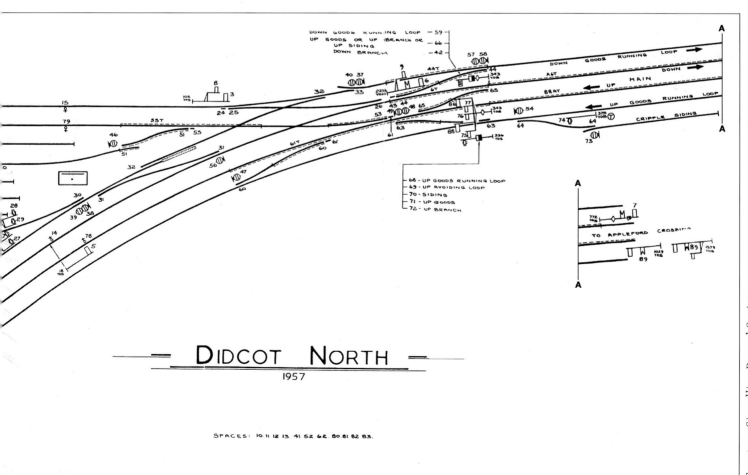

— DIDCOT NORTH —
1957

SPACES: 10 11 12 13. 41 52 62. 80 81 82 83.

Courtesy Signalling Record Society

NORTH AND MIDLANDS TO THE SOUTH AND SOUTH-EAST OF ENGLAND.
VIA BANBURY AND OXFORD.

UP | WEEK DAYS. | SUNDAYS.

	a.m.	a.m.	p.m. p.m.	a.m. a.m.	a.m.				a.m.	
ABERDEEN ....dep					5A15				8 45	
Dundee (Tay Bridge) .... "					7A10				10 49	
St. Andrews .... "					7A13				10 15	
Perth .... "					7A50				12 40p.m.	
GLASGOW (Queen Street) ...... "					7A45					
EDINBURGH .... "					10A 0				2 25	
Berwick .... "				7 A	8A20				4 21	
NEWCASTLE .... "				10 5	1810 a.m.				7 15	
Sunderland .... "				9 31	9A25 p.m.				6 10	
Durham .... "				10 33	11A4				7 43	
Darlington .... "				11 10	1819 a.m.				8 23	
West Hartlepool .... "				9 35	8A55 p.m.				6 50	
Middlesbro' .... "				9 58	10A62				7 30	
STOCKTON .... "				10 8	9A34				7 26	
Thirsk .... "				7 22	9A18				9 13	
Scarborough .... "				10 33					7 16	
Harrogate (via York) .... "			a.m.	11 0					8 5	
YORK .... "			8 17	12 19					10 0	
LIVERPOOL (Central) ....dep			8 10	12 30 2 5					6 20	
Southport (Lord Street) .... "			7 45	9 50 1 12					6 10	
Warrington (Central) .... "			8 39	12 50 2 31					0 49	
Wigan .... "			6 40	10 0 2 16					5A45	
St. Helens .... "				10 0 2 15					5A2	
Stockport (Tiviot Dale) .... "				10 36 2A6					6 32	
MANCHESTER { Central			9 25						7 20	
{ London Rd			10 0	2 15 3 40					6 30	6 50
Fallowfield for Withington and										
Didsbury .... "			9 35							
Oldham (Clegg Street) .... "			9 12	2 2					7 17	
Stalybridge .... "			2 10						6A15	
Guide Bridge .... "			10 11	2 20 3 51					7 42	7 10
BRADFORD (Exchange) ....dep			10 0	35					6 25	
HALIFAX .... "			9 53	20					6 50	
HUDDERSFIELD .... "			10 33	2 13					7 18	7 40
Barnsley (Court House) ....dep			8 20	12 15					6 31	6 30
Penistone .... "			10 50	3 7 4 40					8 23	8 32
Hull { Corporation Pier				11 45						
{ Paragon .... "			7 55	11 38 4 10					6 35	
Grimsby Docks .... "			8 53	1 27					5p55	
Grimsby Town .... "			8 58	1 33					6p 1	
Gainsborough .... "			9 50	2 20					7 8	
Lincoln .... "			9 20	10 5					7 28	
Retford .... "			10 13						7 12	
Worksop .... "			10 27	2 10 8 8					8 15	
Doncaster .... "			9 50	1 50 3A0					6 82	
ROTHERHAM AND MASBORO' "			10 21	2 30 4 28					11 10	
SHEFFIELD (Victoria) ....dep	5 5		11 21	3 29 4 55					9 48	9 18
CHESTERFIELD (Central) .... "	6 0		11 21	3 18					7 50	
MANSFIELD (G.C.) .... "			11 23						10 10	
NOTTINGHAM (Victoria) .... "	5 18	7 57	12 14	5 15 5 59	12 31 12 51 a.m.				10 15	
LOUGHBORO' .... "	5 50			5 27 6 17	10 42 10 22 p.m.				10 49	
LEICESTER (Central) .... "	6 12	8 53	1 48	5 57 6 36	1 18 1 18 a.m.				9 16	
RUGBY (Central) .... "	6 51	9 38		6 26 7	1 0 1 46					
	7 17	10 2	2 16 p.m.	7 21						
Woodford and Hinton { arr	7 45	10 25	2 27 4 15	6 10 7 24						
{ dep	7 52	10 32	2 35 4 22	7 35						
Eydon Road Halt .... "			2 41 4 30	7 43						
Chalcombe Road Halt .... "	8 0	10 41								
BANBURY { arr	8 7	10 48	2 52 4 37	7 6 7 50	3 24 3 2				1 47	
{ dep	8 37	11 7	5 0	7 49	3 44 3 47				1 50	
OXFORD { arr	9 5	12 0	7	0 36	7 5 7 30				12 18	
{ dep	10 2	12 25	4 30 5 43	8 40	7 20 7 55				12 40	
Didcot .... "	10 2	12 52	5 10 6 10	9 30	8 0 8 41				12 40	
Reading (G.W. Rly.) .... "	10 57	1 3	5 5 6 18	9 30	8 0				1 47	
Reading (S.E. & C. Rly.) ....dep	11 15	1 50	6 25 8 15	10 5	9 20				4 10	
Aldershot Town ....arr	12 51	2 58	7 35 9 0	11 11	10 29				5 53	
Guildford .... "	12 53	3 0	7 37 9 21		10 39				6 21	
Redhill .... "	1 55	4 4	8 13 10 33		11 39				8 13	
Brighton .... "	4 13	5 18	11 1		1 6				8 10	
Worthing .... "	4 59	5 50	11 55		2 6				9 0	
Newhaven .... "	4 59	6 33			2 9				9 1	
Eastbourne .... "	5 7	7 37	12 17		2 9				9 1	
Tunbridge Wells .... "	3 15	6 18			3Y15				8 32	
Hastings .... "	1 27	80 5			4Y5				9 27	
Deal .... "	7 21	9 5	2 1		3 45				10 52	
Canterbury (West) .... "	6 31	8 15	1 10		3 35				10 0	
Ramsgate (Town) .... "	7 38	9 10			4 13				10 51	
Margate (Sands) .... "	7 19	9 11			4 15				11 8	
Folkestone (Central) .... "	5 12	8 16	12 50		4 0				9 56	
Dover (Harbour) .... "	7 55	9 31	2K28		4 40				11 30	
{ Newbury ....arr	11K30	16K11	66 0 7K15	8125					7K14	
{ Lambourn .... "		5 8	7 17		9 51					
{ Winchester (Cheesehill) ...... "	12 57	5 30	7 53		9 42					
{ Eastleigh (via Newbury) ...... "	1 16	5 51	8 11		10 16					
BASINGSTOKE { arr	12 35	2 25	5 57 7 30	10 48	9 21 9 27				7 5	
{ dep	12 54	4 32	6 0 7 33		9 36 10 4				7 29	
WINCHESTER (L. & S.W.) ......arr	1 25	5 2	6 47 8 9	30	10 5 10 28 p.m.				8 0	
Eastleigh (via Basingstoke) ...... "	1 40	5 16	7 4 8 24		10 18 10 44				8 18	
Gosport .... "										
PORTSMOUTH (Town) .... "	2 37	6 45	8 49 9 47	12 11	11 4 1 9				10 18	
SOUTHAMPTON { Tn. for Dks. "	1 27	5 34	45		10 38 1 4				9 42	
{ West .... "	1 50	5 46	7 26 6 55		10 56 1 19				9 5	
Cowes (Boat) .... "	3 25	6 55			12 6 3 25					
Newport .... } I.W.C. "	3 55				12 57 3 55					
Sandown .... } Rly. "	5 48				1 0 5 45					
Ventnor Town .... "	1 31				1T8 4 41					
Freshwater (F. Y. & N. Rly.)..... "	6 52				1 57					
Lyndhurst Road .... "	2 18	7 15	9 28		11 17 1 0				9 38	
Brockenhurst .... "	3 4	8 13	9 10		11 33 1 20				9 21	
Lymington .... "	2 59				11 48 1 40					
{ Yarmouth I. of W. (Boat) .... "	3 30				1 20					
{ Newport I.of W.(F. Y. & N.R) "	6F17				3 42					
Christchurch .... "	3 35	6 50	9 10	1 35	11 21 1 56				9 49	
Boscombe .... "	3 11	6 50	9 48		11 30 2 13				9 60	
BOURNEMOUTH { Cen. "	3 49	7 4	9 52	1 46	11 35 2 4				10 22	
{ W. "	5 0	7 25	10 4		11 30					

A Saturdays excepted.   B Mondays excepted.   C On Saturdays arrives Tunbridge Wells at 6.7 and Hastings 7.16 p.m.
D Aldershot North Camp.   E On Saturdays arrives at Tunbridge Wells at 3.50 p.m. and Hastings at 4.43 p.m.
F On Saturdays arrives Newport at 4.32 and Freshwater at 3.52 p.m.   G Via Guide Bridge.   H Via Guide Bridge
and Saturdays only.   J Leaves Oxford at 12.35 p.m.   K Dover Priory Station.   N Via Ollerton and Mansfield.
P Via Doncaster and Rotherham.   S Saturdays only.   T Ventnor (I. of W. Rly.) via Sandown.   Y On Saturdays
arrives Tunbridge Wells at 2.17 p.m. and Hastings at 3.43 p.m.   † The service to the Isle of Wight via Lymington is
subject to alteration. For particulars see special bills issued by the Companies concerned.   § Via Reading.   * Via Didcot
and Newbury.   ‡ Via Didcot.   § Via Manchester (Central and London Rd.) Passengers cross the town at their own expense.

A pre-grouping timetable showing various north-south trains through Didcot.

A Bennett collection

CROSS COUNTRY SERVICES
TO AND FROM THE
SOUTH COAST RESORTS
The whole journey without change!

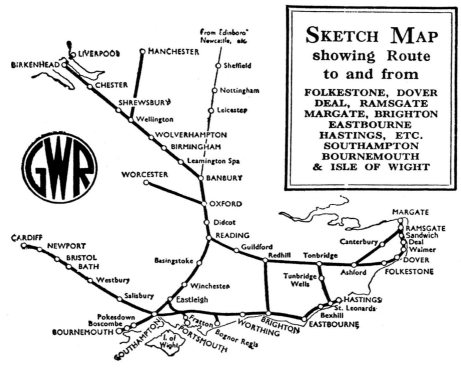

SKETCH MAP showing Route to and from FOLKESTONE, DOVER DEAL, RAMSGATE MARGATE, BRIGHTON EASTBOURNE HASTINGS, ETC. SOUTHAMPTON BOURNEMOUTH & ISLE OF WIGHT

Through Express Services are run by the G.W.R. between the following centres and South Coast Resorts, with connections to and from intermediate stations.

BIRKENHEAD, CHESTER SHREWSBURY, WOLVERHAMPTON BIRMINGHAM, LEAMINGTON SPA BANBURY, OXFORD *and* BRIGHTON, HASTINGS, RAMSGATE MARGATE, FOLKESTONE, DOVER & DEAL	BIRKENHEAD, CHESTER MANCHESTER, SHREWSBURY WOLVERHAMPTON BIRMINGHAM, LEAMINGTON SPA, BANBURY, OXFORD *and* SOUTHAMPTON, PORTSMOUTH & BOURNEMOUTH

RESTAURANT CAR TRAINS
also
CARDIFF, NEWPORT, BRISTOL (Stapleton Road), BATH and WORTHING, HOVE & BRIGHTON

For full particulars see the Company's Official Time Tables and Notices.

WHEN WRITING TO ADVERTISERS PLEASE MENTION "HOLIDAY HAUNTS"

This sketch map in *Holiday Haunts* shows Didcot's pivotal position in the Great Western's network of cross-country services – a tribute to Brunel's foresight.

A Bennett collection

DIDCOT, NEWBURY, AND WINCHESTER LINE. Single Line.

Single Line worked by Electric Train Token between Winchester and Enborne Junction, and between Newbury East Junction and Didcot. Crossing Stations are Didcot, Upton, Compton, Hermitage, Newbury, Enborne Junction, Woodhay, Highclere, Burghclere, Whitchurch, Sutton Scotney, King's Worthy, Winchester.

DOWN TRAINS. — WEEK DAYS. — SUNDAYS.

Distance from Didcot M.	Distance from Didcot C.	Mile Post Distance M.	Mile Post Distance C.	STATIONS.		Ruling Gradient 1 in	B South-ampton Pass.	B South-ampt'n Pass. (Mixed to Winchester)	B Pass.	B South-ampton Pass.	B 3.0 p.m. Oxford to South-ampton Pass.	B Pass.	B South ampton Pass.	A Diesel Car.	B Diesel Car SX	D C'ches.	SUNDAYS B Lambourn Pass.
							a.m.	a.m.	p.m.	p.m.	p.m.	p.m.	p.m.	p.m.	p.m.	night	p.m.
—	—	—	—	**DIDCOT**	dep.	—		X7 39		12 45	3 35		5 52	6 40	8 35		3 0
—	22	17	27	**Didcot East Junction**	pass	—		CS		CS	CS		CS	CS	CS		CS
2	75	14	54	**Upton and Blewbury**	arr.	106 R.		7 45		12 51	3 41		5 58	—	8 41		3 6
					dep.			7 47		12 52	3 42		5 59	CS	8 42		3 8
6	50	10	79	**Churn**	,,	106 R.		7 54		K	K		K	—	—		—
8	35	9	14	**Compton**	arr.	106 R.		7 58		1 2	3 52		6 9	—	8 52		3 18
					dep.			8 0		1 6	3 54		6 11	CS	8 54		3 21
10	42	7	7	**Hampstead Norris**	arr.	106 F.		8 4		1 10	3 58		6 15	—	—		3 25
					dep.			8 5		1 11	3 59		6 17	—	9 0		3 27
12	60	4	69	**Pinewood Halt**	,,	—		8 11		1 17	4 5		6 24	—	9 7		3 33
13	36	4	13	**Hermitage**	arr.	106 R.		8 13		1 19	4 7		6 26	—	9 9		3 35
					dep.			8 17		1 22	4 10		6 29	CS	9 11		3 37
17	49	0	0	**Newbury East Junction**	pass	106 F.		CS		CS	CXS		CS	CXS	CS		CS
17	77	—	—	**NEWBURY**	arr.	513 F.		8 25	SO	1 30	4 18		6 38	7 20	9 24		3 45
					dep.		7 45	9 5	12 35	2 2	4 25		7 20				4 10
19	7	0	0	**Enborne Junction**	pass	199 R.	CS	CS	CS	CS	CS		CS	Conveys passengers off 2.12 p.m. Shrewsbury to connect with 7.25 p.m. Newbury to Trowbridge.			
21	25	2	18	**Woodhay**	arr.	106 R.	7 52	9 12	12 42	2 10	4 32		7 27				
					dep.		7 53	9X16	12 43	2 11	4 33		7 29				
23	45	4	38	**Highclere**	arr.	106 R.	7 58	9 21	12 48	2 16	4 38		7 34				
					dep.		8X 5	9 22	12 49	2 17	4 39		7 36				
25	45	6	38	**Burghclere**	arr.	106 R.	8 9	9 26	12X53	2 21	4 43		7 40				
					dep.		8 10	9 27	12 56	2 22	4 44		7 41				
28	9	9	2	**Litchfield**	arr.	106 R.	8 15	9 32	1 1	2 27	4 49	SX	7 46				
					dep.		8 16	9 33	1 2	2 28	4 50		7 47				
31	64	12	57	**Whitchurch**	arr.	106 F.	8 22	9 39	1 8	2 34	4 56		7 53				
					dep.		8 23	9 40	1 40	2 35	4 57	5 40	7 55				
37	40	18	33	**Sutton Scotney**	arr	106 F.	8 32	9 49	1 49	2 44	5 6	5 49	8 4				
					dep.		8X36	9 50	1 50	X2 45	5 7	5 50	8 6			12† 5	
40	28	21	19	**Worthy Down Platform**	,,	106 F.	8 42	9 56	—	2 51	5 14	—	8 12			—	
42	31	23	24	**King's Worthy**	arr.	106 F.	8 46	10 0	2 0	2X55	5 18	6 0	8 16			—	
					dep.		8 47	10 2	2 1	2 56	5 19	6 1	8 18			CS	
44	27	25	20	**WINCHESTER**	arr. ex G.W.	106 F.	8 51	10 6	2 5	3 0	5X23	6 5	8 22			12†20	
					dep. to S.R.		9 6	10 14		3 7	5 40	—	8X30				

K—Calls at Churn to pick up or set down passengers on previous notice being given at Didcot. The 5.52 p.m. from Didcot calls during the period of daylight only. Guard to collect tickets of passengers alighting.

G.W. engines will work through on these trains {10.14 a.m. Winchester to Southampton. 11.30 a.m. Southampton to Winchester. | 3. 7 p.m. Winchester to Southampton. 4.55 p.m. Southampton to Winchester. | Southern Rly. engine ex Eastleigh for 5.37 p.m. Winchester to Southampton will arrive Winchester at 4.40 p.m.

Southern Railway engine ex Eastleigh arrives Winchester at 4.15—**SX** (for 4.40 p.m. and 11.30 p.m. Winchester to Whitchurch, etc.), and at 7.15 p.m. **SO** (for 11.30 p.m. Winchester to Sutton Scotney.). Leaves Winchester at 12.30 night for Eastleigh

Didcot, Newbury and Winchester passenger service timetable for down trains, commencing May 4 1942, when the route was still single line. All trains were withdrawn in August 1942 while the line was doubled, eventually reopening in April 1943.

ACKNOWLEDGEMENTS

I lived and worked in Didcot throughout the period of World War Two and was under the impression that I had learned a lot of the local lore. It surprised me to find that this was not true when I came to research its history, in particular, that of the railway. As a result I had recourse to call upon several friends to guide me, in particular Kevin Robertson, who, as a renowned author of railway books, steered me through the labyrinth of research without which I could never have started. Then there was my friend of many years, Doug Morton, who pointed me in the right direction to get the best results from Didcot. He introduced me to Willie Pereira, the local photographer who took great interest in providing me with unusual pictures. In addition my thanks go to the Great Western Society for their help, particularly Graham Perry, the chairman.

My thoughts go to the centenarian Bill Inge, for relating so lucidly his memories of so many years on the Great Western footplate at Didcot. I would like to thank all those who in their way contributed or assisted me. Bert East, my driver from many years ago; Larry Crossier for his very valuable contribution on signalling, Ken Ellis for providing pictures and information on Steventon; Brian Davis for pictures; Adrian Vaughan; Frank Miles; David Brown; George Reeves; John Cummings; Laurie Didcock; Oxford County Libraries (Didcot & Oxford); Phil Kelly; Mrs Edna Rice; management and staff of the Public Records Office, Kew; Reading Library; University of Reading Agricultural History Museum; Graham Mallinson for the excellent picture of the old transfer shed showing the broad gauge working. Also Bill Butler for use of his aircraft and my son Barry for flying me to take the aerial pictures.

BIBLIOGRAPHY

E.T. MacDermot, M.A.
History of the Great Western Railway.
Paddington Station, London, 1927.

George Measom,
The Illustrated Guide to the Great Western Railway.
W. Marshall & Sons, Booksellers to the GWR,
Paddington Station, 1852.

Daphne Phillips,
How the Great Western Came to Berkshire, 1975.

Paul Karau, Mike Parsons, Kevin Robertson,
The Didcot Newbury and Southampton Railway,
Wild Swan Publications Ltd.

Adrian Vaughan,
Isambard Kingdom Brunel: Engineering Knight Errant,
John Murray, London, 1991.

Nicholas de Courtais,
The Wantage Tramway,
Wild Swan Publications.

Brian Lingham, Joyce Hall,
The Changing Face of Didcot.

Frank Dumbleton,
Steam Echoes.

Great Western Railway Magazine.

Great Western Echo.

Oxford Times.

Didcot Herald.

Daily Telegraph.

Great Western Railway Museum, Swindon.

British Rail (Western Region) Archives, Paddington.

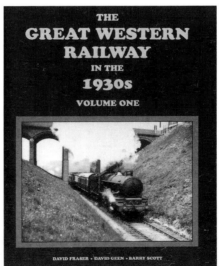